The Rev. Stuart Holt is an Anglican minister and trained teacher who specializes in puppetry. He and 'Higgins the Hare' regularly visit schools and churches to help teach the Christian Gospel. He lives with his wife Angela, and children, Katie, Lucy and Oliver, in Portchester, Hampshire.

▼▲▼▲▼▲▼▲▼▲▼▲▼▲▼▲▼▲▼▲

PUPPETS
▼▲▼▲▼▲▼▲▼▲▼▲▼▲▼▲▼▲▼▲
IN PRAISE

Stuart Holt

Foreword by
David Pytches

Marshall Pickering
An Imprint of HarperCollinsPublishers

Marshall Pickering is an Imprint of
HarperCollins*Religious*
Part of HarperCollins*Publishers*
77–85 Fulham Palace Road
Hammersmith, London W6 8JB

First published in Great Britain
in 1994 by Marshall Pickering

1   3   5   7   9   10   8   6   4   2

A catalogue record for this book is
available from the British Library

ISBN 0 551 02780-0

Printed and bound in Great Britain by
HarperCollinsManufacturing Glasgow

This book is dedicated to my
special family and some unusual friends.
I thank God for them.

May Jesus Christ be glorified,
and may every puppeteer be an
ambassador for Him.

▼▲▼▲▼▲▼▲▼▲▼▲▼▲▼▲▼▲▼▲▼▲▼▲▼▲▼▲▼▲▼▲▼▲▼▲▼▲

Contents

▼▲▼▲▼▲▼▲▼▲▼▲▼▲▼▲▼▲▼▲▼▲▼▲▼▲▼▲▼▲▼▲▼▲▼▲

Foreword

Jesus said, 'Let the little children come to me and forbid them not'. Many of us who have children in our churches are aware that, unfortunately, our manner and method of communicating with them is too often forbidding. Anything that can make the Good News easier to share with children is greatly to be welcomed. Through the refreshing challenge of this new book Stuart Holt will inspire and help his readers to introduce the option of puppets for teaching purposes into the Church. He has described some simple puppets and provides some simple scripts. Stuart Holt is a Church of England clergyman who has previously trained as a school teacher. He also has considerable musical skill. He draws from this combination of skills to provide us with this delightful book. We are most grateful to him.

Some of our own leaders have been using glove puppets in St Andrew's for a number of years. Most of the children come to the front to scrutinize the puppets closely and listen to them intently. We never fail to marvel at those small faces rapt with fascination. In spite of a rich diet of superb images that compete for chidren's attention today, the 'live' and spontaneous puppets still have a major role to play in their godly education.

I commend this very useful book for enhancing the Church's ministry amongst children.

David Pytches
St Andrew's Church
Chorleywood

▼▲▼▲▼▲▼▲▼▲▼▲▼▲▼▲▼▲▼▲▼▲

PART ONE

▼▲▼▲▼▲▼▲▼▲▼▲▼▲▼▲▼▲▼▲▼▲

General plans

Introduction

I am an Anglican minister keen to work with other Christians wherever possible; puppets have enabled me to do this on numerous occasions. Before ordination I was a middle school teacher, and I have used puppets hundreds of times in schools and churches over a period of twelve years. I have only recently received training in puppetry, having learnt most of my skills from practical experience. My motivation for this work has always been to use puppets as a tool for communication, and I have experimented with various methods. I write this book as a lay person, not as a professional performer, and I hope that this in itself will motivate readers to develop their skills, whether they are seasoned performers or beginners in puppetry.

Certainly there are already plenty of books available about the art of puppetry, which provide instructions on making puppets and operating them. This book is intended to offer some guidelines on puppetry based on my own experience, and if you are already using puppets I hope it will reinforce your interest, especially if you have received any opposition from Christians unfamiliar with this form of ministry. For individuals who wish to develop their puppetry skills further than the scope of *Puppets in Praise*, details of courses can be found in the appendix at the end of the book. Many of the people I meet and teach in the course of my work have the impression that you need to be a budding Harry Corbett complete with Sooty glove puppet in order to present a puppet show. They are therefore reluctant to begin, being unaware of what can be achieved with a little instruction, enthusiasm, imagination and prayer.

I first experienced the joys of puppetry on a short course at Ridley Hall, Cambridge, during my ordination training. During our three-day Family Service course an hour or so of instruction was given by Maggie Durran, then of the Post Green Community, a Christian community based in Dorset. It was with great joy that I later presented a short puppet play at Post Green and felt somehow I was returning a gift given to me during my training. Yet all that Maggie had actually done had been to show us trainee clergy the possibilities available. She had issued a number of us with glove puppets, with which we had to present a Bible story. The result was short, amateur and raucous, and moved me very much. Perhaps it was prompted by the joy of all of us being involved, or the foolishness of playing together after a heavy term of theology. A community which can pray and play together has great strength; everyone had been included regardless of background or intellectual ability.

Soon after my ordination in 1987 I was in the not uncommon position of being asked to take assemblies on a regular basis in local primary and middle schools. I further explored the use of puppets to involve the children and present the Bible stories in a way they could understand. I wanted the children to become part of a drama. I carefully put the Bible stories into rhyme, interspersing the narrated stories with choruses which the children could recite. It seemed important that the material for the puppet shows should rhyme, since many traditional shows did. My shows would otherwise develop as they went along. Because of the nature of the assembly presentation, there was little opportunity to rehearse the scripts; children would also be chosen at random to be puppeteers, and quickly learnt to animate the puppets in response to the words. Each show therefore became a unique and creative experience. Out of necessity I had developed a pattern of putting together instant puppet shows to be effectively performed on the spot. Members of my church made me simple glove puppets, small enough for a child's hand and brightly coloured, and soon I had a set of disciples, a Jesus puppet (made from white material), and some OT patriarchs complete with long white beards. The puppets certainly captured the children's attention, to the extent that on occasion they would break into spontaneous applause at the end of the show.

The unrehearsed instant puppet show certainly gives freedom for self-expression, and I have enjoyed some special moments using this technique. During a presentation at an Elim church, one of the teenage puppeteers who was volunteered by his church friends caused us all to laugh as Zacchaeus visibly shrank before our eyes when the fact that he was small was mentioned in the script. On another occasion in a school, the puppet robbers attacking the traveller on the road to Jericho were more than enthusiastic and I had to call them off! The youthful puppeteers certainly got into their parts. The traditional use of glove puppets does enable fight sequences to be very effectively performed, and in such sequences children do become fully involved. It is important to let this develop, at the same time offering an element of control or otherwise chaos can ensue. As the adult, one is very much the controller of the puppet shows and they will develop as far as one lets them.

In the examples mentioned above, we can see how the use of puppets brings a new and vital dimension into storytelling. The written word is fixed and concrete, and in general the end of a creative process. In interpreting a script or story with puppets another creative process takes place. Puppets add to the purely spoken word. In my experience puppets are servants of the written word, responding to it and interpreting it in a way actors cannot. Puppets can do anything in response to a script, an obvious example being that an angel puppet can appear in thin air. My robber puppets actually beat the traveller with their clubs made of drinking straws. Zacchaeus shrank before our eyes whereas a human actor would find it difficult. It is this wonderful freedom puppets offer which gives such pleasure to an audience and also to the puppeteers. We see imagination in action.

Sometimes it is not necessary to have a script read at all. In some Bible stories where there is a lot of action but little dialogue, I simply stand behind the puppeteers and tell them the lines which they repeat after me often to great dramatic effect. More than once a teacher has been delighted that a hesitant child has taken part in this way, and makes a great contribution to the show, where a written script would have otherwise caused the child to 'clam up'. In one particular school, the assembly time was longer than usual when I made a monthly visit and it is no exaggeration to say that a church community grew out of that meeting. The children were keen to bring their parents to a service and we planted a church in the school. Two babies were consequently baptized there, and a puppet show was used to explain what baptism was. So popular did these services become that one parent used to video them to show the children at home.

These puppet shows and scripts which accounted for a small percentage of my weekly contact time with many people were the things on which my prayers became focused. God was doing something quite lovely which led me to develop further what was happening into a strategy for evangelism using my puppets.

In addition to the glove puppet shows, I used my character

'Higgins the Hare', who quickly became a firm favourite with children and adults alike. He is a character a metre in length who hangs around my neck. His mouth moves and he squeaks. No ventriloquism is used. He is always shy to begin with, in order to get a sympathetic rapport with the children (see the shy and frightened script), but as the weeks go by and the relationship develops he gets more and more adventurous and naughty. In common with other puppeteers I use a ritual with the audience. Higgins always arrives in a box with his props and the audience get him to come out by sweetly calling his name. This settles them down and creates an atmosphere of anticipation. After the presentation Higgins goes back into his box to stop the children from playing with him and spoiling the illusion. I never cease to be surprised at the affection children have for him. He has letters written to him and has received presents at the end of term. In this way the puppet becomes a point of contact with the community. When I meet children in the streets they sometimes ask after him and I make up some story for them. Of course this then leads on to contact with their parents and that can be built upon. I have thus found my work in schools to be the quickest way of establishing important contact with people in the community.

I continue to learn more of the joys of using puppets by experimenting with simple ideas. I cannot yet use marionettes, and I am developing my skill with rod puppets. In a very real way puppets are bridge builders between the church and the community. In using them children learn the Bible, and they see the church as their friend. Puppets therefore become instruments by which children can 'reach out and touch'. They like to stroke Higgins and tickle him. Puppets become a point of contact situated in that place between the church building and the world, and as such they are important tools for evangelism.

You may regard puppets as just a bit of fun, which of course they are. But they are also tools for communication and aesthetically pleasing too; cheap to make, and simple to transport. It is surprising too to learn that they are nothing new in the Church. Puppetry was very much part of church life in the fourteenth and fifteenth centuries, and probably they were present much earlier. I like to tell this to those in the Church who are fond of tradition and see puppets as yet another new-fangled idea!

I also believe that anyone can have a degree of success in using puppets. It is important to keep presentation as simple as you can, for if you look for opportunities to use puppets just for effect and a sense of the spectacular, you will find that the message you want to convey will be lost. And it is the Message which we teach which must always take priority when we use puppets in the church.

▼△▼△▼△▼△▼△▼△▼△▼△▼△▼△▼△▼△▼△▼△▼△▼△▼△▼△▼△

2

Developing a plan of action

I trust that you will be keen to use puppets in church but before you launch out into it, it is important to think through what you wish to achieve. Puppets are one way of communicating, and not all Bible stories are best communicated through puppetry. Puppets should be an addition to the proclamation of the Gospel that is already happening in church; if you overdo presentations with puppets you may find them more of a distraction than a help. The puppet show can be included now and again and in this way the show is something special.

We may be inspired with ideas to create this and that bit of drama using puppetry, but as Christians we need to consider where is it leading to, and how is it being used to build people up in the faith of Jesus Christ? My ideas have developed over a long period, and it was only in hindsight that I was able to see how they linked together, when later I taught others how to use puppets in evangelism.

One of the biggest problems I face as a minister of the Gospel entrusted with the task of communicating the truth, is that technology has developed so quickly over the last twenty or thirty years. As a result of this development, children expect instant communication and they can become easily bored. The child of today lives in a computerized age where marvellous graphics keep him or her glued to the screen. Children expect high standards. The fast-moving images on a TV screen present children with an experience which is more exciting than real life. In the world of education the teacher of today has to compete with such programmes as *Sesame Street* which, complete with its wonderful puppetry and animation, presents a very visually stimulating educational experience with, for example, animated letters of the alphabet which have all kinds of adventures. In the world of professional puppetry, puppets now have latex faces and radio-controlled expressions. We cannot compete with these things in the local church and neither should we seek to do so. Yet I am glad to say that there is still a place in children's hearts for the simple glove puppet. Children still respond eagerly to all kinds of puppet shows, and glove puppets are still good sellers in the toy and craft shops. I noticed this especially when I lived in Germany; there are departments in the supermarkets which have large selections of puppets and puppet kits, there are even specialist puppet shops. Much of these are used in playing out traditional folk tales. I would like to see a growing interest in these types of puppets in Britain, which would encourage me to hope that there was some sort of backlash against our video and computer technology.

I am not campaigning against videos and computers, but I am campaigning for creative play for children along more traditional lines. Puppetry appeals to me today because it is so involving. I have not found anything which compares with it as an art, which allows the imagination to be exercised to the same extent.

Because I believe involvement is important, I find when I am teaching Bible stories it is important to involve the children as much as possible in what I am showing them. I look for opportunities to involve all of the audience in the show, and I explain that the audience participation is vital. I also want to get as much information across as possible with the least amount of effort. I know that a child's attention span is limited, so I go for maximum impact. I evaluate how efficient a show is in this. I use puppets because they allow these two criteria, i.e. participation and efficiency, to be satisfied. I evaluate the efficiency of the show constantly. Are the audience involved, are the points of the story retained? I follow the show with a reinforcement of the learning by asking questions about the story. Because puppets are not real people they allow space for imagination in the performance, and each presentation holds the possibility of something new happening. We experience real emotions in assemblies in schools, and this produces life and growth. After one assembly a head teacher said, 'well, that's our drama lesson, RE lesson and music lesson all rolled into one'. The children had learnt a Bible story, they had been free to interpret this by presenting a puppet show, and they had provided a simple musical accompaniment to parts of the action. The story we presented in that case was the raising of Jairus's daughter. The musical accompaniment was provided by recorders and simple percussion instruments. The children who were in the audience had been asked to be wailers who were and are a feature of the Middle Eastern funeral. The assembly ended with a frank discussion about death.

So those are the reasons why I think puppetry is important, and I hope you will share my views. The reasons I have outlined here you will notice are purely practical. I will now go on to explain how you can get down to putting those practical reasons into practice.

When starting out in puppetry things will need to be bought, puppets, props and scenery will need to be made, a portable puppet theatre will ideally need to be constructed. Here involvement is the key. A really exciting way of involving the congregation of a church is in the production of puppet props and scenery, for here are practical ways of involving the church not only in craft activities but also in evangelism. I have found that many in the church can enjoy puppetry, and time, talents and enthusiasm can be freely offered. One church-warden who was a plumber and engineer was delighted to put his skills at the churches' disposal in the construction of puppet theatres and props; he is very talented and is prepared to offer his skills more widely to the church so I have included his name in the appendix as a resource. Another artistic member of a congregation designs and constructs scenery, for example. In almost any congregation there will be those who can sew and design, draw and paint, build and plan. I can't do any of these things.

There are various designs of puppet theatre which are set out in puppet books. We found that an excellent theatre can be constructed from plastic piping at low cost and quite simply. The theatre plan shown at the end of this book was designed to be easy to transport and to store. This has been successfully copied in a number of churches. It has been so designed that small children can stand behind it, or adults can kneel. The theatre accommodates three puppeteers. Scenery can be slotted into the rail at the top. We believe the best material to use for the scenery is artist's foam board obtainable from any art shop, which can easily be fashioned with a sharp knife. The board can be painted or coloured with felt-tip pens. The theatre is constructed from plastic water pipe and the lengths are noted in the plan. In addition to the pipe you will need to obtain the screw fit joints from the DIY store. The whole theatre comes to pieces in under a minute and is easily transported in my Ford Escort estate car. If you can't wait to get on with presenting a show, or you do not want to make a theatre, then a table can be turned over and used for the puppeteers to hide behind. Equally effective is to tie a piece of rope between two badminton poles and cover this with an old sheet. Or you can similarly use a ladder placed

▼▲▼▲▼▲▼▲▼▲▼▲▼▲▼▲▼▲▼▲▼▲▼▲▼▲▼▲▼▲▼▲▼▲▼▲▼▲

horizontally between two stepladders, again draping a sheet over it.

The puppets themselves can be purchased from toy shops when you can find them; but I have already lamented the lack of them, and I have not yet found any on general sale which are suitable for acting out biblical stories. It is much better and much more fun to make your own puppets. Various members of the church have contributed ideas for the puppets I have used. I have used puppets which have been made by old and young. Some puppets have been very simple but effective. A puppet can be simply made from a wooden spoon, the cardboard centre of a toilet roll or kitchen towel, even a paper cup can be very effective. The glove puppet needs to be made in a variety of sizes to fit both children and adult puppeteers. After some experimentation a church member created a very good design which was sought after in the churches, so a pattern was produced, and from this innumerable puppets can be manufactured. These puppets can then be appropriately clothed for animating various Bible stories. There are also some good books available which give a variety of puppet plans, and even people who will help, whom I have come across in my research. I enclose the necessary information in the appendix.

We have a selection of twenty or so glove puppets including patriarchal figures with long white woolly beards, Pharisees in gold braid, and Jesus who is clothed in white. A small group of the committed continued to develop the puppet-making and designing. As the puppet-making group grew it was pleasing to me to hear that they prayed and sang praises as they created. The importance of prayer in all of this is an issue you may wish to explore.

When producing a puppet show, I start the performers off

by giving them a script. From that they develop the action. I believe there is a need to have a script to improvise from. I take the Bible stories I want to use in a service or school assembly, and if possible set them to rhyme. It is this rhyming approach which immediately captures an audience's attention. The rhyming puppet show is a traditional feature of puppetry. I include these scripts with instructions at the end of the book for you to use.

You may wish to dramatize your own scripts or find writers who can do this. A script should be as simple as possible and not involve too many characters. This may limit the scripts you feel able to tackle. If you want to use other scripts you will need to look around. The dramatized version of the Bible is a good resource. I hope you will find the scripts that I have written simple to perform. I believe that it puts people off performing a show if the script is long and complicated, involving lots of dialogue and therefore lots of rehearsal.

Puppets are effective and fun when used in churches. They are of course an art form in themselves, and there well may be members of the congregation who will want to develop this in production of puppets of a high standard. Also some members of the church will no doubt wish to become as proficient as possible in the techniques of puppetry, and will want to attend some of the excellent professional courses run by various puppetry schools. I can see this happening with some of the people I have worked with. However, one note of caution: the better or more professional the puppeteers become, the more difficult it is for the whole church to be involved, as higher standards naturally weed out the poorer puppets, puppeteers and scripts. You have to make a decision about what your aim is in using puppets. It will either be to major on involvement of as many as possible, which builds fellowship but limits what can be achieved, or to recognize that puppetry is an art form and as such only those who are able to develop their talents should be allowed to use puppets in performance. Here it is very much in the hands of the individuals concerned and there is no 'right way' to go about things.

So look at the idea of using puppets as a church idea. You will need to work alongside a committed group who will enable the puppet shows to flourish. A lone wolf puppeteer is not what we're aiming at. Again involvement is the key to success. You will have to enthuse a few to start with. Pass the book around, let people get enthusiastic.

3

Power to influence

As we continue to explore the use of puppetry in the church, we shall need to be clear to define what a puppet is. Here is a problem, for perfect definition eludes theorists, historians, puppeteers and dictionary makers. It is easier to state what a puppet is not. It is not a doll. Dolls are for play; puppets are essentially theatrical in function. Helen Binyon (in *Puppetry Today*) gives: 'man-made actor, inanimate object to which human beings have found a means of giving an appearance of life'. Paul McPharlin (*Puppet Theatre in America*): 'Theatrical figure moved under human control.' Gordon Craig (in *Puppets and Poets*): 'The actor's primer.' Bill Baird (in *Art of the Puppet*): 'An inanimate figure that is made to move by human effort before an audience.' Walter Wilkinson, English puppeteer and author of *The Peep Show* and other volumes, says the idea that puppets are inanimate creatures controlled by human beings is incorrect and that the position is exactly the opposite; the showman is at the mercy of his puppets.

In practice puppeteers are more concerned to create each puppet with its own individual personality, i.e. to give it a definition of character.[1] I would like to offer another definition which describes something of the function a puppet performs and says a little about its qualities. My definition is helpful, I believe, to using puppets in church, as I want to think about the puppet's power to influence:

1. *Puppetry*, A. R. Philpott, MacDonald, London 1969, p.209.

▼▲

A puppet is a character in which we can portray qualities which reflect human nature in its fallen state and its potential glory. This character is used by the manipulator to stimulate the imagination and the emotions of an audience.

This definition is helpful to me as it highlights the power of the puppet to influence for good or evil. How this power to influence is used depends on the beliefs of the manipulator. The puppet is after all a human creation and reflects something of humanity's makeup. A puppet can be the result of a depraved mind on the one hand and the Spirit-filled mind on the other. No pun intended.

For example, if you reflect on some popular puppet characters, you may recall something of each one's power to influence. As you read the names below close your eyes and remember the characters one by one. In this little experiment I have devised try and concentrate on how the characters make you *feel*.

Muffin the Mule (Older readers!); Bill and Ben; the Woodentops; Andy Pandy; Pinky and Perky; the various creations of Gerry and Sylvia Anderson.

These are in the puppet group we can describe as marionettes, i.e. puppets which are moved by strings from above. Is it just nostalgia that makes us smile at our different recollections? What the puppeteers have done for us is to portray before our eyes something of the longings of our hearts, or fantasies. The puppet is able to achieve things that human actors cannot and as such there is unlimited scope for exploration. Just think of the imagination used in the production of the Anderson programmes which are still shown today. I tried this little experiment on a few people I knew. Some of the women I talked to told me that characters such as Captain Scarlet and the Tracy brothers brought out feelings of what I would describe as a 'crush'. Men found Marina from 'Stingray' rather winsome, also some would have liked to be a friend of Joe 90.

There is another major group which we can put under the general heading of glove puppets. Repeat the exercise with the following: Tingha and Tuckha (who were a pair of cuddly Koala bears); Basil Brush (a very English fox); Sooty and Sweep (a type of bear and a dog); Roland Rat; Emu; and the current 'star' of Children's BBC, Edd the Duck. There is probably a favourite Muppet you remember also.

Dwelling on these characters may have brought various memories to light. Hopefully they will bring out mainly feelings of childhood fun and even security. What you also realize as you think about these puppets is that they have personalities and their individual identities which we remember them for. With the advent of TV these puppets have entertained us in our living rooms, they have their own fan clubs, they are big business. They have a certain power to influence the flow of capital. Some of these puppets are international household names. There are few children in the world who have not seen a Muppet.

Over three decades we have witnessed enormous progress in the puppet-maker's skills. The Henson creations have reached dizzy heights of technical perfection. Modern films and children's TV now have quite lifelike puppets and also puppets which are very frightening to younger viewers. There are quite a few blockbuster films which attribute success to the inclusion of puppets. Puppets are also used successfully in the more macabre films; many people are disturbed by ventriloquists' 'human' puppets. The films *The Dead of Night* and *Magic* explore this.

There is no doubt puppets speak powerfully to children. It

is what the puppets are communicating that should concern the Christian. Think for a moment of the Basil Brush puppet. What he did every week in his show was to do what children were not allowed to do in school. He interrupted the story. He was proud, sarcastic and awkward, and that is what we expected of him. Roland Rat became a cult figure for a while in the eighties and was most unkind to his friends and rude to his guests. Pinky and Perky were naughty little pigs, Tingha and Tuckha had their own brand of disobedience. Edd the Duck continues to represent this type of naughtiness at the time of writing. Puppets are allowed to do these things, they bring out the naughty child in us. The only popular recent example of a puppet or ventriloquist's dummy which displays qualities of innocence and vulnerability is the shy duck Orville with the soft voice who brought forth regular 'Ahs' from audiences.

All of these characters are developments of more traditional puppetry found in many societies for centuries. Puppets have a long association with religion, which is of interest to us. In 460 BC Egyptians used puppets in processions to honour Osiris. In 200 BC marionettes were used to portray the two Hindu epics Mahabharata and Ramayana. Stories of gods and heroes were portrayed by shadow puppets. Greeks and Romans used puppets, as did the witch doctors of African tribes.[2] Here the puppets were used powerfully as a means of influence.

We are all familiar with the Punch and Judy show. We find in these stories a variety of emotions; anger, fear and sympathy are all there. The Punch and Judy show actually has a long and interesting history and arose out of the social conditions of the period between about 1760 and 1820. The show revolves around marriage, execution, and damnation, and arose in protest against the social conditions of repression prevalent at

2. *The Puppet and the Word*, R. Sylvester, Concordia, St Louis 1983, p.4.

the time. As such the Punch and Judy show had great power to influence, and the Punch and Judy man became the satirist and social commentator. Mr Punch arose as the folk hero defeating the power of the Law, and the Church as the means of social control. He became the mouth of the labouring poor against an authority which was misused. He even appeared in biblical plays as the character who could outfox the devil. Churchmen became unhappy with his behaviour and he was ousted to the byways and marketplaces, also appearing at public hangings. There are many books and articles written about him; for an excellent account read Robert Leach on Punch and Judy.

When we think of puppet shows what we are experiencing are issues of right and wrong, good and evil, which stir the emotions of the audience. In each puppet presentation there is an opportunity to influence and challenge, and to create nightmares. I still remember the terror struck into the heart of one four-year-old at a secular traditional puppet show, which caused an aftermath of nightmares. What is presented to an audience is a fantasy, yet that fantasy has the power to influence. Here is the power presented to the puppeteer.

This power to influence is seen powerfully in the modern day development of Punch and Judy in the adult puppet show *Spitting Image*. Here personalities are ridiculed to such an extent that we can view them as caricatures. This can bring people down a peg or two, but it can also be dangerous if we don't take people seriously in life because of their puppets.

This power to influence has to be realized if we are to use puppets responsibly. For a long time I underestimated this power. It was demonstrated to me one afternoon in a school assembly. I have a puppet, you will remember, called Higgins the Hare and he had become quite a friend to the children at the school. He was naughty and lively in the presentations I gave and always came out the winner. On this occasion I was presenting a message of how being unkind is wrong. I teased my puppet by offering him sweets then eating them myself. I dangled the sweets one by one under his nose before eating them. I expected the children to laugh. All eyes were on me and there was the silence of stunned disbelief. The assembly ended with my having to apologize to the puppet and retreat to the staff room. A teacher remarked, 'You don't realize the power that puppet has.' And neither I did.

I was really surprised at this power to influence, and had seriously to think it through as to whether this was a good or bad thing. I know I needed to experience the forgiveness of the children, and followed it up in a subsequent assembly with the Lord's Prayer and asked Higgins to forgive me. Fantasy and reality were closely linked in those children. I was dealing with real feelings triggered by what had happened.

What I needed to do as a Christian was to deal with feelings that had been allowed to surface, in the light of Christian truth. The Gospel is to be proclaimed at every opportunity. The fantasy allowed real emotions to surface and the Gospel can speak to those real emotions. This is a great responsibility.

When Bible stories are presented in the form of a puppet play we enter into the realm of presenting truth in a fantasy scenario. Will the child, therefore, in its understanding of life, place Bible stories in the area of fantasy or fairy stories? If this is the case, we would be doing the Church and God no favours at all. We could be accused of weakening the Bible's message, or exploiting it for entertainment. However this could equally be said of drama, Christian painting and the very popular nativity play. The Holy Spirit is the creative Spirit. The Holy Spirit inspired the Bible and has continued to inspire preaching and drama, so why not puppet plays?

The word of God is active and powerful, and where this word is proclaimed, in whatever way, people will be moved.

Puppets can be used as that medium through which the word is communicated, vital, involving and appealing. I would want to say I believe the Bible has the power to influence people; as God's Word it has power. The puppeteer's task is to express that message skilfully, imaginatively and visually. This is not truly possible without serious thought and prayer. Because we are presenting true stories to children, because we are presenting the Word of God, the attitude to the story is different from that of a fairy story. Firstly this happens in the puppeteer, then in the audience. I have always found that children do treat the Bible stories differently from the secular parables I present. Perhaps it is to do with the introduction I give. I hope and trust it is the work of the Holy Spirit, who takes control as the work is offered and surrendered, to glorify Jesus as Lord.

At present I use three main characters when I present a show to an audience. It is the combination of their personalities which I use to touch various chords with the children.

I present a show using a church mouse glove puppet, a red rabbit rod puppet called Roger Rap-it and a caterpillar glove puppet called Clarissa. I call the whole show The Roger Rap-it Show. This in itself creates an atmosphere of expectancy in the audience. I am not proficient enough to present the raps and manipulate the puppet at the same time, so I have some of the show taped.

I assume that the audience knows very little about the Church, I also assume that they know very little about the Gospel, so I have the aim of presenting these in a show lasting around fifteen minutes during which the various characters will be used to influence. I perform this unseen by the audience inside a Punch and Judy type of theatre. At the centre of the stage is a small dummy microphone attached by a shoe lace to a dummy amplifier. Inside the theatre

I have an amplifier/tape player and a microphone on a stand.

The show starts with the church mouse attired in a cassock and surplice coming on to sort out the dummy PA system and to greet the audience. He explains he is a verger and talks about his life in a cathedral. He has become Roger's roadie after a concert in the cathedral and he has been appointed to this task by his bishop. As he sets up the PA he taps the microphone whilst I make popping noises into my real mike. This illusion is funny to watch and adds realism. In this rather strange way the Church is introduced, and the church mouse will have communicated something about the worship he sees in the cathedral. He explains that Roger has also performed in cathedrals. Roger is perceived by the audience as a cool guy who is welcome in church. He is a gospel singer and rap rabbit. The audience cheer as Roger appears. I play a tape of one of his raps, which is of course a Bible story of some kind. Roger then introduces the person who wrote the rap. Clarissa the caterpillar enters; she is shy and described as a changeable character. She's always developing. Roger exits and I play another tape of the caterpillar parable (see scripts). The butterfly eventually flies away and the church mouse returns to ask what happened to her. The show ends.

In this way you can see how the audience has journeyed through different feelings. The church mouse is seen as the link with the audience, a reliable, practical, trustworthy fellow. Roger Rap-it appeals because he's a cool guy; the caterpillar is winsome and lovable.

At the end I appear and talk about God in nature, the Church and the Bible. I use the parable of the butterfly to talk about the fact that we all change and grow. I talk about the life of Jesus and how He died, rose and ascended. I tell them that the church is a place where we constantly remember these things, and we hear the Bible's message in many ways.

I hope you too will use your puppets positively to influence children about your church and your Lord. Don't ever neglect the power of the puppet to influence and use it with all your might and main for good.

4

Communication

As a preacher and teacher I use puppets as tools to communicate. I also use other tools such as visual aids, but puppets are I believe the most effective means of communicating with children that I have used so far. Puppets are primarily an aesthetic experience and expression but they are also very effective teaching tools. Puppets were considered as mostly a play activity, but they are finding popularity in the educational institutions. They are used widely to communicate a number of things throughout the world. They are found in various societies, each finding a definite expression. There is great variety in this. I think it is helpful to us briefly to consider how they are being used elsewhere to communicate. In India for instance there is an increased consciousness about the art of puppetry through state- and national-level efforts. Pani (1985) states that 'Puppetry, which originated and grew up in an agricultural civilization is dying as industrialization is changing the values and taste of Indian society.' The survival depends upon the policy of government to patronize the traditional media and make puppeteers feel important as communicators. This is being actively explored in Indian society as an educational medium for folk education in non-formal situations.

Puppets are advocated for use in Indian society for educational purposes amongst the illiterate, using plays with local dialects. Since no human instructor is visible puppets can present bitter facts. For example, teaching is given on such subjects as the harmful effects of defecating in public, social ethics and superstitions. Puppetry is also helpful in communicating methods of birth control. Research has shown that puppetry is effective in imparting non-formal education. Experimentation continues and it is interesting to note that glove puppets are used. For further information on this important work see *Puppetry and Folk Dramas for Non-formal Education*.[1] The book also contains some puppet designs. I was struck again by the simplicity of the ideas.

Puppets are also used in Africa as communication tools. Closer to home Save the Children use puppets in schools to communicate the difficulties faced by children in poor countries. This is very well received by children and teachers. Save the Children take their puppet shows out to isolated districts of Nepal to use as the means of spreading information about basic health care. Here again we see examples of how puppets transcend cultural and linguistic divisions.

These examples, taken from amongst many, show us that puppets are used to communicate important messages which can make the difference between life and death. The puppet's effectiveness as a communication tool has also not been ignored in the developed areas of the world. Puppets are used in advertising to sell all kinds of products and services. Again I give the example of the Muppets who are used to great effect in education. Programmes such as *Sesame Street* are shown again and again and always hold the audience's attention.

These examples should encourage us as Christians as we too use puppets to communicate the essential message of Christianity. They are effective. We may be a developed nation but when it comes to knowledge of the Christian Gospel most people are ill informed. This is due to many factors, not least

1. *Puppetry and Folk Dramas for Non-formal Education*, Anupama Shah, Uma Joshi, Sterling Publishers PLC, India 1992.

of which is the rejection of Christian values by today's parents. Or rather a rejection of the Church. We realize as Christians that we too have a life-and-death message to communicate, a message of eternal salvation offered in Christ; we too need to transcend cultural and linguisitc divisions to some extent in our society. Puppets enable us in their unique way to attain this goal. The report *Children in the Way* states that learning comes just as much from informal as formal situations.[2] A congregation embarking on a joint project of some sort of puppetry enables all to be involved, and unites adult and child in a common task of presenting a Gospel message. Puppets also cross the generation gap in that they appeal to a wide age-range.

Why puppets are such effective tools for communication has to do with involvement and aesthetic appeal. We learn most from what we see and hear and do. The more of our senses which are involved in receiving information or stimulus the better. Puppets allow this to take place. In no way will they act as substitutes for more didactic learning. I believe that the sermon is essential to our maturing in the faith, and I would not advocate the puppet show as the sole ingredient in the time we call the ministry of the Word. Puppets are used informally to highlight the teaching of the Church. There needs to be a partnership between puppet shows and sermons. All things working together for the building up of the Church and the proclamation of the Word to the indifferent. In the scripts I write for puppet shows I seek to proclaim the Gospel and also to preach. It is also important, I believe, when telling an Old Testament story, to proclaim Jesus as the fulfilment of the Old Testament Scriptures. I do this as a matter of course.

2. *Children in the Way*, Church House Publishing 1988, p.33.1

When using puppets informally to communicate it is important to pick up what the audience is communicating back to you. Good communication is a two-way process. For example, I presented a puppet show as part of a parish weekend and at the end of the show one little boy shouted out again and again as I put my puppets away, 'Jesus has gone!' This in itself communicated a feeling of unease in the audience. We had been teaching that Jesus is always with us! I couldn't let this pass without reassuring the boy of that fact, which was communicated quietly to him with a pat on his hand. Which was witnessed by the audience.

On another occasion when I was presenting a show, a two-year-old was so excited by the puppets he squealed with delight so I couldn't be heard. It was important for us all to enjoy this so I let him carry on; this delight spread to the adults and we laughed for a time before the show continued. In this informal situation we were free to indulge ourselves in fun. This is hindered in a formal situation to some extent.

Church services to many people are seen as formal situations in which reverence is interpreted as being quiet and well behaved. Why do so many people whisper as soon as they get into church? It is real and therefore more reverent I believe to be ourselves in church. Many have found the joy that God comes to us as we worship, then we find we are still in His presence and *then* it is reverent to be quiet.

Jesus of course used a variety of informal learning situations to teach His disciples. He taught them and listened to the feedback they gave to lead them on to the next stage of learning. There was the giving out and the taking in of words gestures and feelings. The proclamation of the Gospel was a matter of seeing, hearing and doing, Jesus was totally open to mankind. We too need this openness to give and receive from God and one another in our churches. It is not the best communication if we simply give out information; we need to be sensitive to what is coming back at us. Puppetry is one of those mediums through which we experience this giving and receiving of words and feelings. The more we do it, the better we become. I think that my work with puppets has helped me to be a better listener and watcher of congregations.

One area I find causes more friction than most in church life is this area of communication. When relationships go wrong there often lies behind the problem some time or other when communication has broken down. This happens on an individual level, but also on a larger scale. We can give out notices on Sunday, we can write notices down on the church notice sheet, and still someone will say, 'I didn't know – no one told me.' Here the minister goes purple in his or her frustration. If you are a minister why not try the puppet notice-giver who in a comical way communicates those often mundane things we all need to know about as a reinforcement of the notice sheet?

It is often in the unforeseen actions which happen in the puppet shows that something is memorably communicated. This happens in a way that is far more effective than the spoken word alone. In the story we were presenting of Moses and the burning bush, I thought that my puppet of Freddie Firefly would help the audience remember the bush. But on the day of its first performance the puppeteer who was animating Moses threw his training shoe over the top of the theatre at the point in the story where Moses took off his shoes beside the burning bush. It was spontaneous and laughter prevailed. At the end of the service I asked the children what they had remembered best about the service; I don't think they will forget that Moses took off his shoes. It was a brilliant bit of communication.

What we have allowed to happen in using puppets is to

create an atmosphere where informal situations can be used and enjoyed. Is that informality welcomed in all our churches? I believe it should be. When an informal event is introduced into the Sunday worship for the first time it is wise to prepare the congregation in advance. A very formal church will need to be taught perhaps that God is just as much in the informal as in the formal events of the service.

In our puppet shows we will always be communicating at three levels. The audience will see, hear and do. What about the other means that we have to communicate? There is the sense of smell. In Catholic worship the incense is used to communicate in this way. I thought of the Bible stories where the sense of smell is mentioned specifically. There are two New Testament stories which are particularly smell-orientated. The wise men who bring frankincense and the story of the anointing of Christ's feet with nard. In presenting these stories a pleasant smell can be released which will make the story more memorable. Then there is the sense of taste. This can be exploited quite easily in stories of bread and wine or fishes. The children can be given these things to taste as part of the show. When presenting the story of the wedding at Cana each child can be given a small glass of grape juice to taste as they become the guests.

We need to think about all of our senses when we are communicating, and so make the things we do in church as memorable as possible. I hope this will help you to think about the way you communicate.

5

Images and idols

I was interested to see a programme on TV which reported on a Hindu who was actively involved in going into schools, and who used puppets to teach children the Hindu stories. The children were greatly interested in this and they naturally became involved in making the puppets themselves and performing with them. It was whilst watching this programme that I realized the importance of taking puppets into schools to teach Bible stories. We are competing with so many other ideologies and religions in today's pluralistic society. We are in fact having to proclaim aggressively the Christian message to win children's attention to Jesus Christ. When we go into schools we are on mission. We are involved in our own way in winning the world for Christ. By 'the world' I take that to mean every sphere of human activity including the part of the world we describe in the broadest terms as 'puppetry'.

The use of puppets in evangelism comes firstly from a deep desire inspired by the Holy Spirit to reach out with the Gospel message. In my experience no one has condemned the use of puppets, and I have used them in a variety of church traditions. The main cause for offence of those within the Church would appear to be images in two or three dimensions of our Lord Jesus Christ.

A fairly recent example of the Church's objection to portraying Jesus as a puppet is when the *Spitting Image* TV programme screened a sketch featuring a Jesus puppet which resulted in letters of complaint to the producer Bill Dare. I spoke with him and he explained that *The People* newspaper took a photograph of the puppet prior to the screening of the programme which appeared on the front page with the heading 'Joke Jesus'. This in itself was provocative to the Church. Bill explained to me that the puppet was in fact a caricature of Mike Rutherford (a member of the Genesis pop group) which they dressed in a white robe. Other newspapers copied the photograph. Before the programme was screened Central TV had received around 500 telephone calls complaining about the idea. After the showing there was little complaint. Bill also received letters and he told me that Christians were complaining about the fact that it is wrong to portray Jesus as a puppet. The Bible was quoted, and some Christians assured Bill of their prayers for him. One lady was so upset by the puppet that she could not get the image out of her mind for some time. A further controversy arose when one Muslim wrote in complaining about the puppet (to Muslims Jesus is a prophet). The *Daily Telegraph* newspaper then published a story that the puppet was later withdrawn because of Muslim protests. This was not the case.

Here again we see an example of the puppet's power to influence. It is this kind of controversy which can offend members of the Church and cause the work of reaching children with the Gospel using puppets to be demeaned. What surprised me was that there were so few complaints from our brethren. Perhaps Christians who take offence do not watch *Spitting Image*.

The task of the Church is to take the Good News of Jesus Christ and communicate that Good News as effectively as possible to individuals through thought and word and deed. We have strong precedents for sharing what we hear of God with others for God is a God who communicates with us.

Firstly He has communicated His existence through His creation; 'For what can be know about God is plain to them (ungodly men), because God has shown it to them. Ever since the creation of the world His invisible nature, namely, His eternal power and deity, has been clearly perceived in the things that have been made' (Romans 1:19–20).

And Jesus took earthly things and used them to lead people's minds to God. He told parables, using imagery that ordinary people were familiar with. In the Old Testament too we read of the prophets communicating the Word of the Lord in visual terms. For example the prophet Jeremiah was told by God to buy a linen belt and to put it round his waist. Then Jeremiah was to hide the belt in a crevice in the rocks. Later he was told to dig up the ruined belt. The useless belt was a sign of the ruin of God's people (Jeremiah 13:1f). The prophet Ezekiel was to make a model of the city of Jerusalem and besiege it (Ezekiel 4:1–3). The Lord showed the prophet Amos a plumb line (Amos 7:7) and a basket of ripe fruit (Amos 8:1), each with special meanings. When Moses was chosen to speak to Israel each sign given to him held a deep evangelistic message (Exodus 4:1–17).

Despite such biblical examples the use of visual aids in worship has been fraught with controversy, not least puppets which for centuries were regarded as idolatrous.

In the Old Testament we read of the idolatry which was prevalent in the peoples around Israel, and everywhere in the Scriptures it is condemned (Exodus 20:4, Deuteronomy 27:15). The image is not reality and it would damage Israel's relationship with God (Deuteronomy 4:16, 2 Kings 11:18). The image of the god to Israel's neighbours served as a means of controlling the god. It was a source of power in the hands of the priest. In the exile to Babylon Israel mocked the making of idols (Isaiah 40:19ff). Also Israel had been terrified of them (Ezekiel 7:20, 8:5, 16:17, 23:14).[1]

---

1. *Dictionary of Christian Theology*, Vol. 2, (Ed. C. Brown), Paternoster Press, p. 287.

The question of idols was still a topic for the writers of the New Testament, and retention of pagan idolatory was a sign of lack of repentance (Revelation 9:20). Paul goes further when he says that there are demonic powers behind idols.

It would be unthinkable for the early Church to have anything to do with images, springing up in a culture where images were immediately associated with pagan cults. As early as the eighth century the debate about the use of idols was on the Church agenda. The iconoclastic (i.e. image-breakers) controversy agitated the Greek Church from 725 onwards, following Emperor Leo III's (717–41) publication of an edict declaring that all images were idols and ordering their full-scale destruction. There was much discussion at this time about the division of Christ's unity, and confounding of his divine and human nature. Some believed that matter was evil. There had been a movement to minimize the human side of the incarnation. Under Leo IV (775–780) the persecution abated. At Nicaea in 787 icons were restored, but iconoclastic events continued until the tenth century.[2]

However, as time progressed the faith was shared in a visual form through paintings and sculptures. Later we find that moving images were introduced into Christian worship. In the medieval Church there were crucifixes which bled and Madonnas which wept. Also there were movable images of Christ and the saints. They would also play a part in religious processions. In English churches there are records of moving images which were part of the church fabric. Well-known examples are: A movable crucifix at Bloxley in Kent, a dove which swept down over the congregation of St Paul's Cathedral at Pentecost, and a puppet play about the

2. *Oxford Dictionary of the Christian Church*, Oxford University Press 1974, (2nd edition), p.687.

resurrection of Christ performed at Witney in Oxfordshire (the earliest recorded puppet show in European history). The reformers purged the Church of puppets as a reaction against superstition. This was often remarkably done and there is a written account of them burning several images at St Paul's Cross in 1538. By such means the puppet shows had their exodus and went out onto the cathedral steps and beyond. Biblical puppet shows continued to be performed outside the Church into the end of the eighteenth century. (For a full list of the biblical plays performed and their dates of performance see Speaight's *History of the English Puppet Theatre*, pp. 325–7).

The question of whether or not puppets are a form of idolatry remains. The debate hinges on the Christian theology of Creation. At the heart of Christian belief is the fact that Creation was good, but became tainted through the sin of mankind. How the Fall actually affected mankind has been the question of debate by many theologians. In regard to the Christian view of puppetry the debate on natural theology in 1946, where Karl Barth and Emil Brunner held differing views, is notable. Brunner held that man's rational nature, his capacity for culture and his humanity remain. Barth, however, argued knowledge of God can only come from God Himself and has nothing to do with man in himself. This is an important disagreement for we have to ask whether God reveals something of himself in the things we call man-made.

Can the creation of a puppet therefore be said to be a sign of God's creative nature? There has been a tendency in the Church in the past to regard anything visual as not worthy of inclusion in worship. During the purging fires of the Reformation, the Church looked to the Scriptures for permission for the destruction of anything the Scriptures regarded as smacking of idolatry. This viewpoint still affects us today.

> Idolatry consists not only in the worship of false gods, but also in the worship of the triune God by images. In its Christian application this means that we are not to make use of visual or pictorial representations of the triune God, or of any person of the Trinity, for the purposes of Christian worship. Historically Christians have differed as to whether the second commandment forbids the use of images of Jesus for teaching and instruction, especially with children.[3]

It has to be said that modern puppets are the result of many practices from which we would want to distance ourselves. The ancient civilization used images in pagan festivals. There is documented proof that what could be described as a kind of puppet was used in this way. A moving statue of a pagan god manipulated by a priest was perhaps a natural development in these festivals. Herodotus tells of an ancient Egyptian custom of parading an image of a fertility god which was about twenty inches high, fitted with a phallus of about the same length which could be erected by strings.[4] There were other statues which moved and would no doubt be used to great effect during the rituals. However, these things in themselves are but objects. What lies behind them is man's imaginative capacity to create something, which is God-given, yet through sin distorted. In the words of the apostle Paul: 'They exchanged the glory of the immortal God for images made to look like

---

3. *Knowing God*, J. Packer, Hodder & Stoughton 1972, p.44–5.
4. Herodotus' works 2 48. Quoted in *History of the English Puppet Theatre,* G. Speaight, George Harrap & Co Ltd 1955.

mortal man and birds and animals and reptiles. Therefore God gave them over in the sinful desire of their hearts to sexual impurity for the degrading of their bodies with one another. They exchanged the truth of God for a lie and worshipped and served created things rather than the creator who is for ever praised. Amen!' (Romans 1:23–25) On this point we find a fundamental difference between the puppets used in Christian teaching and the types of shadow puppets used in Hindu worship. In Hindu puppetry gods are invoked and the puppets and worshippers prayed over. The whole enactment is viewed as an act of worship and the puppets can be said to be a form of idolatry. In Christian worship there is absolutely no inference of this. If we make it clear that any puppet is not for veneration, but is used as a visual aid to understand the Bible stories we may find those opposed becoming more open. In addition when performing a puppet show of one of the stories of Jesus, the Jesus puppet can quite simply be faceless, and this in itself used to teach about the dangers of making God in our own image. I know of at least one quite sceptical woman who was delighted with this suggestion.

In our enthusiasm to reach out and communicate with puppets, let's keep in our minds that in the past the Church has been violently opposed to images. Puppets have been welcomed in the past, and their return after an exile of four hundred years is a reflection of change in the Church. How long this interest in puppets will continue is a matter of interest for us. Suffice to say that at this time there is a great interest in them. Why this is so I believe is the result of several factors which are relevant at this present time.

I would encourage you to think about the issues in this chapter and to pray about them. I hope that you will be able to use your puppets in peace. But do be sensitive to those in the Church who hold views that puppets are not such a good idea.

6

A demand from the church — let's play!

'You're the puppet man, aren't you?' The lady who asked this question was attending a diocesan youth event at which I was helping. I seemed to have acquired a title and I was becoming known by the work I had done around the diocese. I suppose this kind of thing is bound to happen if you are involved in anything which is out of the ordinary, but the question caused me to think deeply about the idea of being labelled as anything but as minister of the Gospel. As I stated at the beginning of the book I am an Anglican minister and not a professional puppeteer. I had talked about my work with puppets with a professional puppeteer who was very encouraging about what I was doing and told me that it was important in the Church. How the work developed is worthy of note for it tells us something of what the Church is looking for at the present time and it puts the work firmly inside the Church. I am not a loner and I do not believe that puppetry is my main area of ministry. It has been an adventure so far for which I am thankful to God, but there have been many times when I have been tempted to stop the development, and I have had to think through deeply whether or not to let it take up more of the time I have. I am, for example, not a naturally gifted writer of books, and each essay I had to submit at theological college was a new agony to be endured. This book has been written largely in the dead of night after the other duties of a Church minister have been fulfilled. You will no doubt find that your puppetry will take the place in your life which you assign to hobbies. That is why I have in part opted for simplicity.

You probably haven't got a lot of time on your hands.

I was recently reading Karl Barth on Church dogmatics. I had been led to read him with regard to his views on natural theology which were relevant to my work on puppets. He writes about the passion that Christians have to honour God and how the passion to share the Gospel can be expressed in other passions. My passion for puppets I realized was really another avenue for the passion I have to teach the Bible to anyone who will listen and look. As such I can only conclude that it is a good thing, and I believe it is a passion which is God-given. I liken the experience to the question I was asked at ordination as to whether I was sure as far as I knew my own heart that God had called me to be ordained. I find confirmation in the calling as I get encouragement from the Church, in other words as the ministry is accepted. So too the Church has been the source of confirmation of the puppet work. This has been my source of guidance.

I was taking a family service one Sunday and during the service a puppet show was presented. It was a very simple message. Afterwards a member of the congregation encouraged me and asked if I would be prepared to use the puppets more widely. I replied that I hadn't really thought that anyone else would be interested, besides there surely were many people using puppets in the Church. I contacted some puppeteers to find out what they were doing, and I realized there was little resourcing for the minister who might wish to start out in puppetry and would require some simple encouragement and a few scripts. I saw Gos Home the following week. Gos runs the Christian Resources Exhibition. I received a telephone call asking me to exhibit my work. Gos was most insistent and believed that puppets were going to be well received by the Church. I told him I would think about it. I talked and prayed with Christian friends and received further encouragement from Colin Reeves, the editor of *Christian Herald*. George Hicks, the artist at Herald House, encouraged me to publish independently a booklet of scripts. By a coincidence I met the printer who was a friend of my sister. So the booklet was a possibility. It was all typed by George's wife Jane and produced in a week. I contacted another friend we had made through a funeral contact, who was a clothes designer. She produced puppet plans which could be used like dressmaking patterns. A small package of simple-to-use resources was produced for the exhibition and the catchy name 'Puppets in Praise' was adopted. It all happened very quickly.

Before CRE I visited a photographer for some publicity photos I had been asked to provide for press releases, and Gos produced a feature which appeared in the major Christian papers. Colin also featured the puppets in the *Christian Herald*. It was with a sense of adventure that I went off to CRE. I'd been asked to step out in faith. The night before the exhibition I prayed and wondered how the idea would be received by the Church. I was no businessman, and here I was with a collection of puppets and my book of scripts and four puppet plans.

During the exhibition I was surprised by the interest in 'Puppets in Praise'. I had to keep reprinting order forms. I covered my costs and gave away over 800 order forms. In the first day I knew this was something people were interested in. The real encouragement was that so many people from so many denominations were united in their enthusiasm to reach young people. I received lots of encouraging words from those who visited my little stall and still get regular letters asking for materials. I was also featured on local radio and I had a lot of fun. It was then that I was approached by my publisher and was asked to write this book.

Following on from this I have been asked to lead services and training days on the use of puppets. This has been a source of great joy and a great privilege. 'Puppets in Praise' is rooted in and encouraged by the Church. If so many people are interested in this area, and no doubt other areas of creative art, why aren't we seeing more of it? I now believe Christians are to take initiatives in these areas and I only tell this story as a testimony to what I believe God wanted of me at a particular time. This I hope will in itself encourage you if you are in a position to try out an idea. The interest in and desire for puppets is coming from the Church and I believe this is a sign of the prompting of the Holy Spirit who brings a common mind. I believe there are reasons for this at this time which I mentioned in the last chapter and which I will now share with you.

Technology has so advanced that we are now enjoying lots of high-tech fun. I recently enjoyed an evening out with our youth group as we played at laser warriors. But there is also a price to pay for this advancement. Computer games and game shows with marketing giants behind them have recently escalated. There is even a super Mario Brothers film. Children are spending hours in front of the computer screen or the TV. There are recent studies on this. There is unemployment which is in part a result of the development of technology. Families are continuing to break down at an alarming rate. There is a feeling of isolation in our society. Our creativeness which is part of our God-given humanity always seeks an outlet. I believe that it is in the Church where things can be addressed from the Word of God and where we can be free to offer back the creativeness we have to our Creator in worship. There is also a total reorientation of the Church to 'family worship'. This takes various forms in various traditions. This is what I believe the Spirit is leading us to explore. With this movement there is a vacuum of ideas for expressing creativity in worship; What can we do in these family services? I believe that God is inspiring us to play. The idea of a God who wants His children to play together is perhaps a new one to you. Yet I have a picture of the loving Heavenly Father who likes to play. He planted this desire in us, after all. We remember with happiness the homely family things which held high priority in the homes of our grandparents and which are noticeably absent from the homes of the nineties. Home-made entertainments which unite us in fun and laughter and song are even absent from our children's parties. How many parents lack the ability to play or provide environments of fun? Even birthday parties are handed over to burger bars to entertain children with fast food. I observed one such party and the girl in charge seemed to lack this ability herself. Simple things we can all take part in and grow through are becoming scarce. Have we so sadly lost our ability to play or are we lazy? The Church is fast becoming one of the few places where we can truly experience the joy of family fun. Play is part of celebration. Apart from the artistic beauty of puppetry there is that undeniable sense of homely simple comfort. Puppets teach us but they are also uniting us at deeper levels leaving us with a lasting memory of joy in church. Far from pandering to the world the puppeteer is working against the isolation and breakdown in today's society. This is a very important point. I also believe that there is healing in this as relationships are developed.

How long this interest in play will be highlighted in our church services is up to us. In playing together we are deepening our relationships with one another. One of the earliest signs of a breakdown in a child's relationship with its friends is the common statement I heard most days as a teacher: 'He won't play with me any more.' We have the challenge set before us of using our creativity to God's glory, for the building up of His people, and that will involve sacrifice and hard work. An atmosphere for play needs to be created, a loving atmosphere in which there is security. Puppetry helps this to happen. Puppets in the church can be a real expression of love for God, His Word, and one another. 'Dear children, let us not love with words or tongue but with actions and in truth. This then is how we know that we belong to the truth, and how we set our hearts at rest in His presence whenever our hearts condemn us. For God is greater than our hearts and He knows everything!' (1 John 3:18–20). Puppets proclaim the truth in action and the stories they tell are our stories. They help to create an atmosphere of rest in God's presence. Laughter in church is a sign of that security which the Christian knows in Christ. John goes on to say that the one who fears is not made perfect in love (1 John 4:18). John concludes his letter by exhorting the Church to keep away from idols (1 John 5:21) which are fearsome. If puppets are not of God for His children we would not experience the joys of shared fun and the building of fellowship.

Underpinning all of this is the work of prayer. I encourage you to pray about the puppet shows you will perform, and make that prayer informed. We are to bring before the Lord the breakdown of relationships and ask Him to use us and inspire us to bring His message and His joy in all we do. Remembering the puppets' power to influence we can use this most effectively to teach family themes. If we pray that God will give us a real passion and zeal for using puppets we can look forward to a change in our attitudes.

As I use puppets with the very young and their mothers I am always aware that our times together of singing and laughter are one huge opportunity of experiencing something of the family fun God wants us all to know. And the faraway look of regret in some parents' eyes is the beginning of that recognition of things being not as God would have them in their lives.

I have rediscovered the pleasure of play through the puppet work. For me this in itself has been a therapeutic experience. I have had to learn to use my imagination, I have experimented with different types of voices for the puppets and I have shared my times of playing with others. I have naturally been led on to play with children in the church, and experienced regrets that I had not played more with my own children. I have even been encouraged to play in my prayers and I realize that I have grown in my understanding of God as my Heavenly Father. This is a real blessing which I have found from all that I have done with puppets, and a blessing I would want many more to experience. In some deeper way I have come to understand Jesus's words that if you do not become like a little child you cannot inherit the Kingdom of Heaven. The desire for play and the ability to play are part of life in that kingdom.

I am not saying that we are like puppets which an omnipotent God wants to manipulate. That is not the Christian understanding. God does not manipulate us, we have free will. We enter into a relationship with God as our Father through faith in Christ. The Abba Father prayer which Jesus taught us implies a relationship of trust, and love in which there is no fear. Only when we are confident of His acceptance of us are we free to enter into the joys of puppetry in the playful way I have suggested. If your church fellowship doesn't laugh together perhaps it's time to address where the fears are lurking.

7

Methods of presentation

I have experimented in churches and schools with methods of presenting the Bible stories using mainly glove puppets. What I have continued to develop over a long period of time is a particular method of presenting a puppet show. The methods I now use have been developed with two main aims. Firstly I really wanted to find and use a format which was the most effective when used in communicating the Bible's stories to children. I wanted a method which could be easily used so that it would involve the whole audience wherever possible and so allow the maximum opportunity for participation. Secondly the method should be simple to use and therefore some kind of routine would be helpful, not only for my own sake in explaining to children what I wanted them to do but also for the children themselves to understand and to feel confident in what they would be asked to do in the course of a puppet show. These aims led me to explore various methods of presentation to an audience, some of which of course were less effective, usually because they were too complicated or required puppetry skills that the children just didn't have. Experience had taught me that if I was to involve others in a show and it was to be a success, some kind of script was needed for the puppeteers to work from. If you are working from a script you feel that you have something concrete on which you can base the animation as there are words which are written describing the action in the show. In this way improvisation is actually enabled as the puppeteers act out what is being told to the audience. There are various methods you can use in the creation of a script. Each script is unique and as such it will require a different interpretation by the puppeteers. There can of course be scripts where the puppet characters have been given set lines to perform. Some Bible stories can only be interpreted in this way so that the audience are clear in their minds as to who is speaking in the play. This type of script can be written quite easily by taking a Bible story and writing it so that the various characters tell the story by speaking in turn as in the Bible story. However, I have found that if you want children to be able to do this, quite a bit of rehearsal will be required beforehand or you will end up with a very poor show, perhaps inaudible to a large number of the audience in a large setting as the children are crouching behind a theatre and they have not been instructed in voice projection. It is much better therefore to have narrators. The narrator is able to read the script giving it full attention, whilst the puppeteers can give all their concentration to animating the show.

I am still continuing to develop the idea of writing rhyming scripts based on stories from the Bible. The script is read by a person who is a confident reader and stands between the audience and the puppet theatre; this ensures that a point of contact is kept with the audience at all times. In the scripts, I have written choruses for a small group to recite, and these have been carefully thought about as they highlight the main points of the story, or are taken as literal quotes from the Bible. The small chorus of children who have volunteered are told to recite this chorus, and then the audience are instructed before the show begins to repeat everything that the chorus says in the course of the show. I have found this simple method to be very effective in use as it lends itself to involving everyone in the show.

The children's attention to the show is further engaged

through the script by the rhyming and rhythmic nature of the storytelling, and they are expectant and interested or 'kept on their toes' as they are encouraged to listen carefully for the part I have told them they are to repeat. This type of repetitive teaching method of course is nothing new – repetition and rhyme is a very old teaching method and children have for centuries made up their own playground rhymes which have their own regional variations. Rhyme is very much part of childhood experience. A rhyming puppet show is also a part of the traditional presentation in puppetry in many parts of Europe and it is interesting to read other puppet scripts for comparison. Many puppet shows which we have access to in puppet books do rhyme in strange ways, as for example in Punch and Judy. From the point of view of the time you have to present the show, often with no previous rehearsal time, I have found that this method of puppeteers, narrator, and chorus, is very simple and effective to use. With the permission of the head teachers I have tested out my scripts in school assemblies with the children having had no previous preparation for the show. This type of rhyming script presentation is good because it enables each of the Bible stories to be heard for the first time by the audience and the puppeteers. The scripts and the puppetry are therefore new and exciting to everyone; each show is a fresh show. As the children in the audience see the shows being performed and the drama begins to unfold before their eyes with their schoolmates helping to animate or to read, they too wish to be involved in the presentations. Hands start to shoot up when volunteers are asked for. Each puppet show presented in this way also becomes a new and vibrant creative experience with a real feeling of 'anything can happen'. Even when I have performed the same script a number of times in different places with widely varying audiences, and even though I am very familiar with it, I am never bored in the shows which are presented as something new always happens. There is a great joy in working with puppets from a script; you see the script being spontaneously developed and interpreted as through new eyes.

There is another method which I find effective and simple to do and this is to perform a 'wide' puppet show. This is where different characters in the show are placed in various parts of the hall or church. This enables wide-scale fun and makes unusual use of space. One thing I soon learnt was that even if the puppet was seen to be placed on the end of someone's arm, the children still looked at and interacted with the puppet, appearing to be oblivious of the puppeteer after a short period of time. The puppeteer too was often so engrossed in the animation of the puppet that the person seemed to forget they were actually standing up in front of a large number of people. I still find this phenomenon fascinating. I am aware that this experience is quite a common one amongst puppeteers. To present a show with no previous rehearsal, I simply stand behind or beside the puppeteers and feed them lines which they repeat, often hamming it up to the delight of all. All of this helps to make things memorable for those involved and that I believe is a good thing in itself. Again no preparation is done beforehand. Each new performance is a fresh and creative experience.

Yet another method I have explored and I use occasionally, especially in church services, is to tell the congregation a puppet parable using my own larger puppet Higgins the Hare. This is again a different method as it does not specifically involve others in the performance so it is more of a solo presentation. Looking for variety I have now added a church mouse to the puppet characters I use, so that the children feel there is always something new to see, and he comes out at church festivals such as Harvest, Easter, and Christmas to teach church year themes. When performing with this kind of puppet you really do have to have some sort of performing skill, I believe. If this puts you off the idea and you are thinking 'I could never do this', then be encouraged from my experiences that with a little practice, determination and confidence, you may well surprise yourself and your church congregation.

If you would like to develop some simple techniques to use such a larger-sized puppet and if you are starting off, then you need to acquire a puppet of your own. You can get a puppet either from a toy shop, you can make one, or get someone else to make one from a pattern as I have already mentioned. I know that Children Worldwide for instance supply various patterns and their address is included in the appendix at the end of the book. You will also need some sort of script to work from which you must practise and memorize; either use one of my scripts or write your own. A good place to start from when writing a script is with a strong theme such as anger or fear or love etc. Now you need to become familiar with what it is you want to say, and placing the puppet over your hand address your talk to it asking if it agrees etc. When you start off on this adventure you will probably find it difficult to animate the puppet and it will appear lifeless or awkward at first. Try to keep the puppet moving about, using simple movements at first, looking at you as you speak to it and also get it to look into a mirror which is your imaginary audience. One of the tricks that I use I learnt as I went along and that is whilst I am talking and developing a story, the puppet will stare open-mouthed at a member of the audience. Children do seem to like being noticed and they love the idea that the puppet is looking at them; it seems to communicate that they are in some way special. As an aside in the script you can ask the puppet what he's looking at and tell it to pay attention to the story like the children. Also I occasionally get the puppet to look up whilst I am talking and the children obviously notice this and some eyes will also turn upwards and as I turn to the puppet I do the same, shrug my shoulders and carry on with the telling of the story. These little ideas may seem trivial or silly but they are simple to do and rather effective in keeping the audience wondering. They also add to the fantasy that the puppet is alive and doing its own observation. You no doubt will devise your own particular styles and jokes, and there is unlimited scope for imaginative manipulation; your puppet may for example have a habit which your audience will become familiar with. If you really get enthusiastic and want to make the most of this kind of puppetry then watch professionals on the TV. You may also go to a course run by puppet schools such as the London School of Puppetry. I learnt a great deal on a one-day course I attended.

I have a few set talks I use in churches and I can recite them verbatim, and it is true to say if I'm comfortable and confident with what I'm doing then the audience are comfortable and that allows for more effective communication. I have had a few disasters, of course, and the congregation has let me know where I went wrong, but that is how I learnt. I am also a trained communicator as I qualified as a teacher. Good communication I believe lies in saying a thing simply, so you need to be absolutely clear in your mind as to what it is you want to say. I have also found through experience that you can never be too extrovert in your presentation; puppets are larger than life. By nature I am not very extrovert. Indeed, when I perform the 'shy and frightened' sketch, it is me who sometimes feels like this. I suppose I must project this into the puppet, so the audience are really getting quite a lot of me in the performance. I expect you will find the same. The naughty puppet that you present to the audience is really a part of you which you are presenting. The angry puppet, the puppet which perhaps sends up our religious pretensions is really you even though you wouldn't dare to say the things the puppet says or do the things the puppet does. And here is another important aspect of puppetry; these furry little characters we use can get away with saying and doing so much more than we feel we can, and here is a freedom to explore without causing offence by being in any way vulgar or cruel.

Puppets can be used in church to do a variety of things, they can for instance make announcements or encourage the children to come to Children's Church. They can add fun by appearing at church social events and so on. But I think there are boundaries we have to set, lest in our enthusiasm we make serious mistakes. A puppet is not a real person and should not lead worship or preach or lead prayers. A puppet should not preside at a Eucharist even in the course of a script. A puppet should not pretend to have a conversion experience or be involved in a baptism service or a funeral service. All of this sounds like common sense but I think I am warning about profanity. I was challenged about these things at a Diocesan Eucharist where Roly Bain presided as a clown with exploding offertories and other clowning activities, and to see him praying the Eucharistic prayer as a clown was a shock to many. But underneath the clown personality is Roly who is a real person and an ordained priest. The puppet is quite a different matter as it represents another separate person. Please don't let the puppets near the Lord's table as this may well cause offence in the church which is not helpful to your cause of using puppets in worship. Puppets have no place in the ministry of the sacraments.

I hope you will find these few simple guidelines helpful and really a matter of common sense, and that you will be encouraged to carry on practising your art. You will find that the scripts I have included in this book will be relatively easy to perform, and from them I hope you will be encouraged to write some yourself. One important note on scriptwriting – don't be tempted to veer away from what the Scriptures actually teach for the sake of getting a rhyme or making a personal point, and wherever possible quote the Bible verbatim. If the audience can be encouraged to repeat vital parts of the story (as in my scripts on Zacchaeus and the temptations for example) this has a good effect in reinforcing learning in the story and we are in fact learning our Bible verses in a rather covert way. It is the improvisation of the puppeteers which also so often reinforces learning in quite unlooked-for ways. I mentioned a performance of 'Moses' as an example of this. At the point in the script where Moses was told to take off his shoes, the puppeteer threw a training shoe over the top of the theatre! The effect was visually stunning (blink and you miss it) and in the sermon we picked up that point from the story. Later the children still talked about it. They remembered.

These then are the three simple types of presentation I have to offer you, and I hope you will find much success and blessings in store. The blessings I have received are a greater love for God's Word and a greater zeal to proclaim it. Many of the scripts were by-products of fairly detailed Bible study and came after I had preached on them. If they are successful in their performance it is because the Word always bears fruit, I believe. If you also believe this and are prepared to let the word speak to you and change you then you will share in the blessings the Lord has prepared for His people. I remember always that the Lord resists the proud and gives grace to the humble. Are you a humble puppeteer? Who do you want to exalt in your puppetry? If you are going to use puppets because you want to be noticed, or even to impress your church with your skill, you will find limited success. Do take this to the Lord in prayer, and talk to your pastor if necessary. Be sure that any selfish motive will be exposed for what it is. A puppeteer is a servant of the Word in church, not someone who is using the Word for personal glory. In this context a pastor may well ask you how you are serving the body of Christ in other ways, so before he does so why not ask that question of yourself?

8

Variety

Once you have begun and as you go on in using puppets to tell Bible stories in church, you will, I think, want to explore and experiment with techniques and ideas, and here again you will find some whole new areas of delights are in store for you and your audiences. There are some excellent books which are generally available which you can either buy or order from the library on puppetry and its various techniques, so I am not going to go over ground that other authors have covered or to repeat what has already been published on the art of puppetry, except to provide one practical idea by supplying a puppet theatre plan for you, which will cost you or your church around £25 to make. The materials which you will need to obtain to make the theatre are easily available from DIY stores or builders' merchants. Use this as a starter for other more adventurous ideas of your own which may be larger or smaller theatres. I am not aware of any other book on puppetry which has been published which shows how such a theatre can be constructed.

With regard to the puppets which you will use in the shows that you present you may wish to be adventurous and to make marionettes which will require some degree of competency in basic craft techniques. Marionettes are not easy to operate effectively and they will require of you more than average skill in your manipulation. Professional puppeteers spend a lot of time practising with the marionettes. I spent ages trying to get one to walk in a realistic way; I'm sure it had a mind of its own! Also the method of manipulating marionettes for performance is an art form, but do be encouraged to have a go and do make a point of trying to go and see a professional marionette show. It will I am sure delight and inspire you to attempt some ideas of your own, but be aware that quite a number of these professional shows can be disturbing to young children as the puppeteers deal with adult themes which can have an element of fear in them, or they may of course present some ideas involving magic or witches and monsters.

To explore further the variety of types of puppets you may also wish to experiment with shadow puppets, which because of the contrast in light and dark in shadow, becomes an excellent medium for dealing with the passion of Jesus where glove puppets cannot be manipulated effectively. One of the gospel accounts of the Passion of Christ can be read by a narrator whilst the shadow puppets seem mysteriously to animate the story you are presenting. Of all the techniques that you could use to present the Passion I think this is a very memorable way of presenting this very sobering part of the gospel story to children and adults alike and I believe that it is a far more effective method than using actors in a drama of the Passion story. The shadowy figures are very powerful tools in the hand of the manipulator. The methods of shadow puppetry are described in shadow puppet books, and in some more general books on puppetry, and of course we know that in Indian society the Indian puppeteers traditionally use this method very effectively in storytelling. Traditionally the Indian puppeteers will use naked flame to light the drama, with simple oil lamps being used. You may wish to do the same or to use candles or battery-operated torches, or even opt for an OHP which is usually available in church. But remember to experiment with the position of the light source and to engage the help of a director to stand and watch the show and to comment on its effectiveness. Some form of screening may be required to darken the performance area. These shadow puppet shows obviously lend themselves to evening performances. In your celebration of the Easter message in what is commonly called Holy Week a shadow puppet presentation can be put on. Good Friday evening is I believe an emotional time when such a show can be presented with great effectiveness.

Because of my interest in puppetry I am asked from time to time to present a training day on the use of puppetry in the church. I led such a training day recently which was well advertised by the sponsors and as a result it was attended by a variety of Christians, mostly with a little knowledge of puppetry ranging in churchmanship through Anglican, Roman Catholic, Pentecostal, Baptist and Methodist. Some had travelled long distances to attend the day, showing a great enthusiasm for puppetry. All were keen to explore variety in methods of puppetry. On this day we focused as a group on the use of junk puppets. Junk puppets are self-explanatory but to clarify this they are puppets made from common household items. Ten Bible stories were presented as complete shows after just an hour's preparation in small ecumenical groups. The ingenuity of the puppets' designs which were created on the day was a real inspiration to us all, and the day will be remembered as one of laughter and inventiveness in script-writing and interpreting scripts with puppets made of simple objects. The puppet designs which were created were varied, and the puppets were imaginatively and artistically con-structed from such things as egg boxes, toilet rolls, plastic bottles and cereal packets. Here we could see and use puppets which could quite easily be made at no expense and thus further add variety to the presentations by allowing the participants to use their imagination and their artistic skills to the edification of all. They also experimented with the use of space. Puppets were constructed in a range of sizes, the smaller ones were even portrayed with squeaky voices. So the type of puppet used actually affected the dialogue which again added variety to the shows.

One thing which I have come to realize will greatly add variety to an effective puppet show is the use of music. I have included some songs which I have written to use with the shows which you present. You may of course use these as you think fit, and perform the songs with the help of church musicians or of course you can use well-known Christian songs as well. Taped music is most effective in presentation, and the puppets can be animated to appear to sing along to the songs. If you are very adventurous and you work with a team with musical talents you can put together a short puppet musical which could explore a particular theme in life or a Bible story.

Puppets are relatively easy to transport and simple to set up in a variety of places. They are interesting and people are generally fascinated by them and are willing to talk to the puppeteers. Also few people are needed to put on an effective puppet show as one person can portray several characters in a way that no human actor can. It seems obvious therefore that puppets are great news for street evangelism. What, however, will really draw a crowd around a show is music. People really gather round to the sound of music and the Gospel can be very effectively proclaimed in the open air with a sense of vibrancy. Be bold in this and with a small team of puppeteers do try a script with music out in the high street on a shopping day. The script that you use should be short and punchy with a clear, well-presented message and it can be repeated at intervals during a half-hour period, after which time you move on to another location. Other members of the church who are committed to this stand by, each furnished with the details of where and when your church is meeting. Puppets in this context are being effectively used as bridge-builders to the community. I know of Christians who have a vision for street work and are very committed to this idea of taking puppets on the road; I think it is a great thing for the youth of a church to be involved in. But I must give one note of warning – if you do take your puppets out onto the streets and you are using copyright music, it is proper that you should have a licence to do this. This will cost £59.42 plus VAT per annum. The licence should be obtained from the Performing Rights Society and if you write and explain what you are doing they will advise you. I think it would make this book more worthwhile if I at least do encourage you to get out of the church building and out into the streets where the people are waiting to be talked to about Jesus. This is a message echoing in other areas of church life these days and by other church people. Why not be a puppet pioneer in this area? Remember that Jesus taught and sent his disciples out into the roads and byways challenging people to respond to God's love for them.

One less obvious area of life in which you can use puppets is in pub evangelism. This is an area I have most recently become interested in as the puppet work progressed and I became more proficient. I have been involved in a variety of pub work as a secular entertainer, in Christian missions to a neighbourhood and also lately as a minister. These days, remembering the popularity of the *Spitting Image* TV show which is aimed at adults, there is already a receptive puppet-minded public sitting in our pubs ready to be entertained. Admittedly this is not an area of evangelism for the naive or for the inexperienced youngster and some pub evenings can become quite hostile. My youth group turned up unexpectedly to support me one evening and I was placed in the difficult position of having to send them home. But the early disciples went to people where they were and today the popular walks organized by 'The Walk of a Thousand Men' are exciting and inspiring. To produce *Spitting Image*-style puppets requires some degree of expertise. Latex puppet kits could be obtained from the National Puppet Centre at Battersea or you can make sponge puppets. The Puppet Centre at Battersea does have a video for sale to the public which explains how to go about this. Before you go into a pub you will need to chat to the landlord whose permission you will obviously need to put on an evening show and who may well be pleased to let you perform especially if you tell him that you are going to bring some extra customers from the church!

When you go to the pub do take plenty of church support with you (we outnumber the regulars by three to one). It's also a good idea to take a package of secular entertainment along with you. To achieve this, why not get the church music group to practise and to put together some popular songs which everyone can sing along to, and to arrange the music which you are presenting into sets of five songs with a pause of half an hour between each set. In the intervals which you create in the evening at the pub church people can mingle and chat and witness at the bar explaining why you are there that evening. In these planned intervals a simple thought can be presented through puppetry in a talking head format, that is, two or more puppets having a conversation. The Smith and Jones model of talking heads developed by Mel and Griff is a good one which people are still familiar with and it has been copied by other presenters, and little thoughts about ultimate questions in life can be introduced into the evening. Themes can be discussed and adopted for the evening such as 'Is there life after death?' This is something everyone wonders about whether they profess a faith or not. The puppet show allows you to get away with so much more in the pub. On a few occasions I have stood up and spoken to people in pubs and I don't mind admitting that it is a daunting task to do so. The puppet is I believe a way forward for the Church to challenge people in the pub without seeming pious or self-righteous. The puppet fits the setting so well. And of course as entertainment in itself it is a memorable experience for those who see it. The puppet script you use can even be recorded and played back on a powerful tape machine and the talking heads can be animated, appearing to converse with one another. The landlord may well be very keen for you to return, and I believe the landlord may want to be associated with the church. One landlord remarked to me after an evening in his pub, 'Church people are such pleasant customers and they don't cause trouble.' We are after all bringing salt and light into the places where we witness and this in itself is an important aspect of the work wherever we go.

One Christmas we were asked to put on a carol concert in one pub after first putting on a skiffle and blues evening. There was the God-given opportunity to preach and I responded to this with the encouragement of the church people. After a similar skiffle and blues evening in another pub the landlord wanted to collect money in the bar for the church. The money was given to Help the Aged. As a church we didn't go with any view of financial gain, as people usually assume this is what the church is after, and we made this clear. So why not pop into the local? You may well find some quite unlooked-for blessings. The work builds up the reputation of a church in the community and relationships are forged which are steps on the way to faith. Puppets help this work of befriending at the local pub.

Once you start looking outwards to the local community you realize again the enormity of the task God has given to His Church to go and make disciples of all people and of course it's all on the doorstep. In the pubs, on the streets, in the hospitals, in prisons, schools and clubs . . . the list of venues you will think of is seemingly endless for your puppets, and really of course your church, to pop into. Indeed I think these are places we should be involved with as a matter of course, but what gives new impetus to go is that there is a presented acceptable mode of entry to these places. The puppet show is the attraction, in the eyes of the world, and the Church is in fact using puppets as the point of contact with the community as it did in centuries gone by when puppet shows presented religious stories to a largely illiterate populace. And I think again of Mr Punch who was at the heart of British social life in days gone by, and I realize that our puppets can also be used to challenge real social problems and to speak out for the Church. God speaks in so many ways to so many people. He after all created variety, and it should be the aim of the church puppeteer to express a rich variety of modes of presentation.

Another joy we find in puppetry in its variety is that it crosses social and racial barriers quite naturally. As such it is a wonderfully socially uniting art. It is also one of those many things which churches can be seen to be doing together and there is another important bridge to be built. I have used puppets in a variety of denominations and always the response is the same, unity. There is that unity which comes when you present something as a team with a clear message to proclaim. There is that unity which comes to people when they laugh together.

When I started out in the ministry I never imagined that God would use something as simple and indeed as foolish as puppetry to unite Christians in the proclamation of the Gospel. It is perhaps a timely reminder that God transcends all boundaries (even though we erect them). He even uses foolish things to bring us His joy and to spread the foolish message that we proclaim in the eyes of the world. For when we make and animate our little puppet it seems such an ineffectual little thing, made as it is of cloth and card, and we realize that in ourselves we can indeed do nothing great for anyone of any eternal significance. But we can ask Him to lead us out and to give us courage and inspiration to use the variety of talents and gifts He freely gives us, as we share the Good News of His love.

9

Mums and toddlers groups

I have worked with several mums and toddlers groups and I have found that here is a good place for puppets to be involved, indeed perhaps one of the most natural places. When I started this area of outreach I must admit I was at a bit of a loss for words, not to mention courage, when I visited them. Here was an area of Church life in which I felt very inept. I had no preparation for working alongside these mothers, and my experience as a father of three children was all I had to go on. The days when I used to bounce my children on my knee were long gone, and I thought I was rather out of touch with the needs of young mothers, and added to this I was aware that many of the children I met had no steady father figure at home. I have become involved with this area of Church life purely through the invitation of the leaders of such groups who were members of the congregations I have ministered to. I have found that the groups each have their own spirituality and expectations of the minister and you have the privilege of sharing with them in their world all the joys and frustrations of motherhood. I will briefly describe the differing situations I have encountered and how puppets have aided my relationship with the groups.

I ministered for a while in an Anglo-Catholic congregation, and the weekly contact I had with the mothers and toddlers was based around an informal Eucharist. Here my role was simply that of presiding at Communion sitting amongst toys, toddlers and mothers. After some thought I used soft toys and my puppet Higgins to present simple stories to relate more effectively to the children. This captured the attention of even the smallest tot. What the puppets actually achieved in the group was to unite us all in talking to the children. As the puppet came out of the box the mothers would encourage the children to look and engage in conversation together about what the puppet was doing. On many occasions I simply brought the puppet out and the mothers did the talking; after all they had the necessary skills in this area. We majored on simple themes; shyness, naughtiness and such like. As some of the fathers of the children were away from home regularly due to the nature of their work, this theme emerged quite naturally in our table talks and so opened up areas for prayer and insights for counselling. Here I came to realize that the puppet was being used as a catalyst for expressing latent feelings. The puppets allowed for freedom within a structured sacramental service to express fears and doubts, and of course the joys of life. The puppet was also used to allow for explanation of what the Eucharist is. I would explain to the puppet what we were going to do and the mothers would follow suit by teaching their children about the Communion service. I found these times very rewarding and from that group I received my first set of glove puppets for acting out Bible stories. I learnt a great deal there.

I also have visited play schools and simply taught Bible stories using puppets; these had no connection with the church and were real opportunities to bring the Gospel message. From such visits I found that the major Christian festivals were ideal opportunities to go in and present the stories with puppets.

In an Evangelical-tradition parish the role I adopted was quite different. The toddler group was very large and my input was one of a link between the church and the community. My aim was to befriend and use the puppets as a set activity to present the Bible. Young children were able to be involved through finger puppets and simple glove puppets, although to a limited extent. All the activities built up a level of trust and expectancy in the group. Again the major festivals were the place for presenting the Christian story. We decided to hold three special services a year, a Harvest service, a Crib service and an Easter garden service.

THE HARVEST SERVICE

The children made a large frieze out of pieces of pasta, pulses and corn. This was brought into the church, and in a simple presentation Higgins the Hare had explained to him what Harvest was all about. A short period of singing followed, and we closed the service with a short prayer of thanks. The service lasted twenty minutes and was followed by a harvest lunch.

THE CRIB SERVICE

Here we were on familiar and traditional ground; everyone had their own expectation of what a Crib service should be. The Crib service has a long and interesting history in the world of puppetry. In Germany cribs with moving figures were so common that the term *Krepche* (crib) simply signified a puppet show. Our figures were made out of weighted plastic bottles suitably attired and made by a grandmother of one of the children. There were three groups of figures: the Holy Family, the shepherds with sheep, and the wise men with camels. The stable was made by a keen father. The children processed the figures around the church and up the aisle and eventually we all gathered around the crib for the singing of 'Away in a manger'. It was surprisingly moving. Here is a script

which can be used for such a service, a narrator reading as the
action takes place.

The story we are going to hear
Happened long ago,
An old story but ever new,
It's a story we all should know.

Here come Mary and Joseph. (Procession)
Look! can you see them?
Travelling along the road,
They're going to Bethlehem.

Mary is having a baby,
In the town there are no spare beds,
All the homes are full of guests,
They stay in a stable instead.

In that little stable,
With very little fuss,
Mary gives birth to her baby,
And she names him Jesus.

On the hills the sheep are grazing,
Shepherds watch with crook and rod.
Angles appear! How amazing!
Singing Glory to God.

The shepherds now make a journey (Procession)
To find baby Jesus the King.
As they go on their way on this glorious day,
Listen to the song that they sing.

(Tune: Baa, baa black sheep)
Baby Jesus lying in the hay,
We are praising you today.

We are the shepherds, we want to sing
Glory to God for baby Jesus the King.

Now we see some wise men (Procession)
Coming from afar.
They have travelled many miles,
Following a star.

They're bringing special presents,
To offer to the King,
And as they go to Bethlehem,
Listen to them sing.

(Tune: Twinkle, twinkle little star)
Twinkle, twinkle God's bright star,
Guiding wise men from afar.
Presents we have for the King,
Gold and perfume we now bring,
Twinkle, twinkle God's bright star.
Twinkle, twinkle from afar.

Here the action is complete and all the figures are in place. The service can end with 'Away in a manger'.

THE EASTER GARDEN SERVICE

Here again the Church has used puppets to tell the Resurrection story. There is the well-documented story of Jack Snacker of Whitney, a comical puppet figure who sees Christ rise and lets out a strange clacking sound; this puppet play dates from around 1500 and is the earliest recorded European puppet script. This information may in itself inspire you to explore a script of your own. I simply use Higgins the Hare to explain all the parts of the Easter garden which has been made by the group. The service then concludes with some songs ('God's not dead', 'Jump up and down', and 'Father God I wonder') and an Easter egg hunt in the church followed by tea.

There have been many joys in these services, and I am convinced that the adults learn a lot from them about the faith. One lady had not been into a church before, another had attended once as a Brownie; they were moved by these simple services and there was a sense of wonder on their faces. Puppets I believe do communicate a sense of wonder on occasions. There was also demand for a monthly afternoon toddler service. We called it 'Pushchair Praise'. The interest in this service was greatly increased when a number of mothers and their children took part in a puppet show. The one presented was 'Zacchaeus' and I made the point that he was not a good person, but Jesus loved him. I asked for volunteers to help and one lady did so. Afterwards she expressed interest in attending church and a basics course. In that afternoon session she was welcomed and involved, and began the journey to faith which called her to belong to the church. In a puppet show you can do these things, creating the opportunity of belonging, leading to believing.

I am convinced that puppets are a vital part of working with these types of groups, and they have helped me enormously to overcome my own awkwardness in relating to them. Here is an unexpected bonus to puppetry from the minister's point of view.

Toddler groups are more difficult to work with as the children are so small. They want to be into everything, and the puppet theatre and the puppets themselves are all open to exploration. The only way to perform successfully a puppet show in a small hall is to enlist lots of help. Many of the smallest children will not understand the stories but they are fascinated by the movement of the puppets. The Gospel message is actually being presented to the mothers. What is being communicated to the child is that this is fun and Mummy is laughing. The church man is a fun man, a man to be trusted. Over a long period in a parish church this trust is to be built upon as the children are incorporated into the life of the church. Also in the puppet show most of the child's senses are being used and this is stimulating. Why not think about this as you present the puppet shows for small children. The children can see and hear of course, they can reach out and touch a furry puppet. Why not perfume the puppet as well so they can smell it?

FORMAT FOR A 'PUSHCHAIR PRAISE'

Theme: A time to decide what you want your child to believe.

Introduction: We meet at a new time. It is a time when our church is doing new things.

Singing time: 'My Grandfather's clock was too tall for the shelf'

'If you're happy and you know it clap your hands'

Puppet time: The rap from Ecclesiastes chapter 3 'You Gotta Wait' OR a puppet play of a kind where the character is waiting for something, for example going to school.

Reading: Joel 2:28–32.

Short talk: During this the children are playing with toys.

Explain that God promised to pour out His Spirit in the last days. Explain that Christians have come to realize this. Also explain that God has appointed a time when the earth shall end.

Question: What is a Christian? Would you want your child to be a Christian? Discuss in groups over tea or coffee.

Song to end: 'Father God I wonder' by Ian Smail. Children join in with shakers. (Tins filled with rice, etc.)

Skill and worship

I had just finished a lively family service on the theme of Zacchaeus the tax collector, and we had looked into the fact that Jesus changed his life so he could again show generosity to others. I had been invited by this church to conduct a puppet show and to preach; the church was a very warm fellowship and they were keen to encourage a Christian brother with an idea which attempts to cross the generation gap and the denominational boundaries. It had, I thought, been a great family time and the fellowship was very encouraging towards me. I was asked to stand at the door to shake hands and to have a chance to meet the congregation albeit passingly and I was kept busy saying my goodbyes. Whilst I was doing this, a helpful young member of the congregation, wishing no doubt to be of assistance to me, dismantled my puppet theatre. When I had finished my farewells and I came to load the puppet theatre into my car, I realized it was dismantled in all the wrong places. In short it had been broken. A wave of sadness swept over me, and that showed on my previously smiling face, and the young man was a little embarrassed. It was not that the theatre had cost a lot of money, in fact it was very cheap to put together, and it was donated by our churchwarden who had constructed it with much precision and skill. What I was upset about was that it had been treated carelessly, in fact it was my negligence and oversight in not giving clear instructions which caused the mistake. There are other things like this that have happened in church involving bits and pieces which have been made and brought in for the services. I remember for instance on another occasion when I had used the glove puppets in church, and some of the children were playing with them after the service in a way which would have led to their destruction, in fact one puppet was being pulled in opposite directions by two eight-year-old boys. I rebuked them for this and they apologized as they realized that this behaviour was definitely out of order.

This leads me on to what I would call setting standards in what we do with puppets in church, for your standards also communicate something about you as a puppeteer. If you are careless in what you do with your puppets this will be communicated, believe me. The puppets and props and paraphernalia which you will accumulate will need to be properly looked after when the presentation is finished. This is however so much more than just common sense. There are I believe some very good biblical reasons why we should place a value on the things that we use in the puppet shows. Those people who have made the puppets and have spent time and used imagination and skill in their design, and who have chosen carefully the exact materials to make the puppets, who have spent hours sewing and embroidering, are to be recognized for their skills which have been given to God. To abuse deliberately those things which have been made carefully is something which can cause hurt to those who have given of themselves. I have come to place a very high value on the skills that people display in the service of God and of others. I looked into the Scriptures to understand this better and there are a few references to skill in the Bible.

We believe as Christians that it is God who is the true Creator of all things and this is recited week by week in the creeds in case we forget. The Christian revelation realizes that everything was made through Jesus Christ and what is more everything is to return to Him. He is the Son and heir. At the beginning of John's gospel and similarly at the beginning of the letter to the Hebrews we see this set down clearly for us. With reference to the skill we use in God's service, it is to the Old Testament we look for evidence of God enabling and inspiring His chosen ones to make something skilfully for His service alone.

In the book of Exodus in chapter 31:1–11, we read of Bezalel of the tribe of Judah being filled with the Spirit of God to become skilled in making all kinds of things for the worship of God. There is quite a list of the things he was skilled in, notably Bezalel was given craft skills and artistic skills. These skills we read are to be used to the glory of God, and are a sign of His Holy Spirit at work. Today with the Spirit of God being emphasized in much of our teaching and church practice, we should remember that what we call creative arts are also a sign of His presence and anointing in a believer's life and therefore these skills are of special interest. They are further signs to us of God's presence with His people. Puppet-making which is a skill is also I believe a sign of His anointing and presence, as is the skilful manipulation of puppets – especially in the puppet shows which show a recognizable level of skill. If we see and recognize skill in God's service it is to Him that we direct our delight, not to the puppeteer. The puppeteer is not looking for praise from men, but wants the glory to go to God in everything.

Having said this we must also say that there are some things we might engage in with puppets which are not skilful. An 'anything will do' attitude does nothing to glorify God, indeed quite the opposite. It is interesting to read the next chapter in Exodus and we find that after God appoints His skilled workers there is the well-known incident of the golden calf (Exodus 32). Here was something that was not made for the

▼▲▼▲▼▲▼▲▼▲▼▲▼▲▼▲▼▲▼▲▼▲▼▲▼▲▼▲▼▲▼▲▼▲▼▲

service of God, indeed it was an idol they made when they became faithless. I find it interesting to read that it was not made skilfully. Aaron explains that he simply threw all the bits and pieces together and out came a golden calf. 'So I told them', says Aaron, 'Whoever has any gold or jewellery, take it off. Then they gave me the gold, and I threw it into the fire and out came this calf' (v24). Here is something that was just thrown together with no thought of God. It seems to me we stand in a similar position to the Israeiltes if we just throw things together in a puppet show or indeed any other area of worship and expect Him to bless us anyway, or worse we end up looking to the puppets as cheap entertainment. The Israelites were manufacturing an idol, and many of today's idols are quite carelessly brought into existence. Sometimes we are tempted to look to the things we think we can create for our comfort, and we forget that God is our only true comforter. He gives the inspiration for using our ideas to glorify Himself. It is in this glorification of God that we can find comfort.

But I wonder how many golden calves are still being manufactured quite unskilfully in our worship? If we are to take this idea of puppetry seriously in our worship we should expect to offer that which is worthy of Him, in short only our best is going to be acceptable in His service. If we are skilled in some way then let's do everything to be more so for the glory of God; we will find in this a deeper and more meaningful performance, realizing that it is the Spirit who is our real inspiration in offering creative abilities to God. He will not inspire anything that does not glorify Jesus. So we need always to have that question in our minds as we decide what to present with puppets in our churches. 'Does this glorify Jesus?' I only raise this point because not everything done in Jesus' name does this. We know when something has been done carelessly. The puppet show should not in any way demean Jesus by, for example, proclaiming something about Him which isn't true. We need the gift of discernment in this, and we should have our work tested by other mature Christians. Moses saw the idol the Israelites made for what it was. A carelessly constructed image around which there was ribald behaviour. Whilst there may be fun and laughter around a puppet show, there should also be an awareness of God amongst His people. I have learnt as I have presented shows that I have at times presented a careless piece of work, and God by His grace and through His Church has shown me that the Spirit will testify when it's been edifying to the people.

When we realize that skill is important in God's service, we find the impetus for all kinds of creative art workshops in our churches, and the motivation to go out and attend courses which will better equip us to give God the best. There are Christians who run puppetry courses which are very worthwhile and of an exceptional standard. I encourage you to get in contact with the London School of Puppetry whose address I include at the end of the book. Here are Christians who are professionals, having worked on TV and with the Henson puppets, who are people the Church can be in contact with. The cost of a day course will be more than worthwhile, and discounts are sometimes available.

I attended a day at the school, which currently uses part of the National Children's Home in Highbury, London. I was challenged to look at puppetry as an art form, and the training involved quite an effort of concentration and was quite tiring emotionally and physically. I realized there were a lot more skills to learn, and it helped me to be sensitive to those who are professional puppeteers and are very concerned about standards. There are other schools of course, but I know these people are committed to enabling the Church. I also learned that not all puppeteers who present religious puppet shows profess to be Christians even though they are skilful. There is much we can say about this, but in terms of evangelism I would say that they too were inspired by God, even though they would not say so in those terms. A shared skill or interest brings the Christian puppeteer into contact with those who are also skilled but have no faith in God. Here bridges can be built.

So I return to my feelings which I expressed earlier about the misuse of puppets and props. These have been skilfully made for God's service, and as such I believe the Spirit was inspiring and enabling the creators. I feel I am to be a good steward of these things which have been set apart for the Ministry of the Word. They have value, as art forms in themselves of course, but they are to be used as tools for teaching so a fair amount of wear and tear is to be expected. However negligence can lead to abuse. I advise you also to show a bit of care in simple ways such as returning them to a box after use.

In the same way care should be shown to the puppets which have been made by children. The finger puppet made by a small child can be enthused over with the child. A real interest can be shown in what has been achieved, and a sense of worth and inclusion can be communicated to the child, in that the puppet is to be used and seen in church. Children respond to encouragement, and what seems to you to be a very simple thing is valued by the child who made it. Children love to have 'something to show'. Our attitude to a child's creativity is important in other areas of church life too. I am sad when children have produced a model or a picture in their Sunday school or club and come into church with a screwed-up, dog-eared bit of paper. What that communicates is anything will do, it's only church work, which we can fail to address. This can lead to the torn and doodled-on Bible, and I don't think I go too far when I suggest the doodled-on church wall can be a result of lack of care in this area.

Behind all of this is the truth that skill is to be used and developed in God's service and for His glory. We are to recognize, develop and encourage skills in ourselves and in our brothers and sisters in Christ. There should be no sense of jealousy or rivalry between those involved in exercising skills. So often there are jealousies in the body of Christ and the person who is exercising a skill can be threatening to the person who has not yet found a place of service in the church. Puppetry is just one small area of the use of skill in God's service and takes its place amongst so many others. The puppeteer like other skilled people in the church is always open to the temptation of pride, and therefore needs to exercise the gift under authority. Humility in someone's life will clearly be recognized, and if this is combined with skill, the puppeteer will not I believe go far wrong in using puppets in church.

11

A plan for running a puppet day

Because of my interest in puppetry I have been asked from time to time to run puppet days for churches, and they have each been unique experiences from which I have learnt and have received encouragement. If you want to launch puppetry in your church then a Day is a good way to do it.

The advantages of a whole day are the reward for the planning and effort you will put into it. It is common sense that the more you plan ahead the more you will achieve, so take care in preparation and be sure of what it is that you really want to achieve in your day. The first thing to do is to pray and to become very familiar with the Scriptures you want to look into. With this in mind you can define your broad aim.

Broad aim: To become familiar with the Scriptures.

Find the Bible stories you want to use, read them, and then ask the Holy Spirit to help you understand what the Scriptures are actually saying. What is the major theme which emerges from the story? Is there clear moral teaching, for example, or is the story an event which has been recorded such as a healing or a miracle. If you can obtain a commentary on the Scriptures you want to explore this will be a good help to understanding the main theme of the passage. Next, try visualizing the scene which you have read about. Imagine you were actually there, what do the people look like, and how do they react in the story? What is the main action in the story, what kind of movement is there, do some people move more gracefully than others, for example? Having visualized the story, imagine how this would appear as a puppet show. Where would the characters stand, how many of the characters would you include, would the crowd be presented or not? Then use your imagination to look for the unusual in the story. Is there a character you could use to tell the story to an audience?

Having explored the Scriptures in this way you will have done a fair amount of mental exercise and I hope this will be beneficial to you. You have also gone through a process which is quite lengthy and will help you to explain to others how they in turn can explore the Scriptures for themselves. To select stories for use in your day, I suggest you choose one story to six people, so, for example, if sixty people are coming to your day you can have ten stories to look into.

Next you need to decide what it is you actually want to achieve in the day. These shall be your aims. The aims of your day would be, for example:

1. To produce ten scripts for puppet shows.*
2. To make puppets.
3. To perform the shows.

Now you are clear as to what it is you actually want to achieve you can plan accordingly. Here is an outline of your plan which if followed should enable you to minimize stress for all concerned. I have found that most stress and friction in churches is the result of poor preparation and lack of communication. Follow these guidelines and you are a long way towards a successful rewarding experience.

1. Submit your idea to the church leadership for approval. This can then be shared with the PCC or elders for

*Assuming that you have sixty people.

discussion. Already by this process the church can get a picture of what is going to happen.

2. Set a date for the day no less than six weeks before you plan to put it on. Select a venue and book it. It will most probably be a church hall.

3. Communicate what you want to do. Make sure it appears in the church news-sheet and in the church notices. Get an artistic person to make a poster and/or handouts. At this stage decide if you want to invite other churches. If so, liaise with their leaders. From this make a list of those who want to come with their addresses.

4. Start collecting materials to make puppets. Ideas for junk puppets are included at the end of this chapter. Get the church to bring in the junk for your day and set aside a place (which may be your spare room) for the junk to be stored.

5. Assuming you have sixty people obtain ten cardboard boxes from a supermarket in which you put the junk. Label each box with the Bible story it will be used to present. Groups will work from these boxes.

6. Get at least one Bible per group of six people.

7. Organize food and drink. Are people bringing a packed lunch; are you providing tea and coffee?

8. Make the puppet theatre described in this book, or another book on puppetry, or set one up by draping a curtain or sheet over a rope tied between two tall stepladders. It should be large enough for three people to fit behind.

9. Make four glove puppets, one out of white material. (Plans for glove puppets are available in puppet books or in a sheet format from Children Worldwide; see appendix.)

10. Set up your hall ready for the day. Get there at least one hour before the day begins. Make sure you have time to pray.

▼▲▼▲▼▲▼▲▼▲▼▲▼▲▼▲▼▲▼▲▼▲▼▲▼▲▼▲▼▲▼▲▼▲▼▲

The Day. 10 A.M.–3 P.M.

10 A.M. Welcome and prayer. Worship.

10.20–11 A.M. Presentation of puppet shows. Explain that you are going to present some puppet shows together and it is going to be fun. With the group present the following puppet shows:

1. A cuddly toy show: Use the script of 'The Lost Sheep' and get volunteers to act out the drama as you narrate; remember to pause as the action takes place, allow laughter to develop. This will break the ice for everyone.
2. Perform the script of 'The Stilling of the Storm' using a cardboard cut-out boat and your four glove puppets, the white one is to be Jesus. Split your audience into rain, thunder and wind. Ensure they all go absolutely quiet at the words 'Be still'. In the silence be sensitive to the mood; you may feel it is right to sing 'Be still' or to say a prayer.
3. Perform the script dying and rising. Either someone reads it for you (having practised) or you have it recorded on tape. This is a very different show as it is a solo performance.

   Invite feedback on what you have experienced together as a group. How do people feel? Do they feel more united now than at the beginning of the day?

11 A.M. Coffee break.

11.20–12.30 Split into groups of six. Give each group a Bible story to consider. Give each group at least one Bible. Don't let them choose the story. Each group is to elect two people to be scriptwriters. These will also be narrators. Or one narrator can be chosen. Get one person to read the story a few times in the group and the members are to go through the process you did all those weeks ago, so be sure to explain it clearly. Pray for the Holy Spirit to inspire you all. After at least ten minutes ask one member from each group to collect the box with their story labelled on it.

Explain they are now to work towards producing a puppet show for performance later in the day. Two scriptwriters are to work on writing the script, and the other group members are to be engaged in making the puppets. To aid this you can copy the designs at the end of the book and make them available to the groups. If this is the case add it to your 'things to do' list so that they are ready on the day.

12.30–1.30 P.M. Shared lunch.

1.30–2.00 P.M. Final practices in groups. Wander round and encourage people as they practise their animation.

2.00–3 P.M. Show time. Allow each group to present their puppet show to the others. Allow time for feedback after each show and be positive in encouraging the participants. Explain that now the group members will be able in turn to teach children this method of junk puppetry as they have experienced it for themselves. End the day with prayers of thanksgiving.

These are Bible stories which have been successfully used in such a day and which you may wish to use. I add notes on the creative ideas people had in the presentations and which I feel are helpful. But don't let this limit you in any way.

Suggested Bible stores; Labelling for the boxes:

1. Noah; Genesis 6:13–14, 17–22
                  7:7–10, 17–24
                  8:6–12, 18–22

In this story supply something the group can make an ark with. A cereal packet is helpful.

2. Daniel; Daniel 6:6–11, 13–24
   If you include an old egg box or two the group can make some wonderful lions.

3. David and Goliath; 1 Samuel 17:1–11, 32–51
   Include a long cardboard tube from a kitchen towel roll and the inside of a toilet roll; these will make very acceptable puppets for David and Goliath.

4. The entry into Jerusalem; Matthew 21:1–11
   A long cardboard tube, some pipe cleaners and a plastic cup will enable someone to make a donkey. Perhaps the donkey can tell the story.

5. Parable of the sower; Luke 8:4–15
   Here the story might be introduced by two naughty ravens.

6. The good Samaritan; Luke 10:30–37
   A selection of toilet roll centres will enable the group to construct the puppets that will be needed for the show.

7. The wedding at Cana in Galilee; John 2:1–11
   Provide at least six plastic drinking cups and one of those green gardening stakes to join them together with.

8. Jonah and the big fish; Jonah 1:1–17
   2:1–3, 8–10
   The big fish can be constructed out of various materials, sponge or foam rubber, for example.

9. The big catch of fish; John 21:1–14
   Make sure you include an old onion net. Silver foil or sweet wrappers are great for the fishes.

10. The crippled beggar; Acts 3:1–10
    If you use drinking straws for the crippled man's legs, you can design a puppet whose legs straighten before the audience's eyes.

These ideas have come through preparing and performing these puppet plays with churches. I hope they will give you some inspiration to make a start in your puppetry. Be confident and have fun. Trust God.

School assemblies:
Attainment through puppetry

As I have stated previously, I have used puppets in schools to communicate effectively. For my part the puppet shows provided an effective means of communication and the children responded to this. They looked, listened, participated and *enjoyed the puppet shows*. The feedback I have received from head teachers has been very encouraging, to the extent that the work with puppets in schools has been welcomed at county Education Authority level. I have worked particularly closely with a head teacher who is herself a Christian and as a result of this we are able to offer concrete suggestions for fulfilling attainment targets in the National Curriculum. I write this chapter as encouragement to head teachers, class teachers with National Curriculum responsibilities, and to clergy or Christians working in schools as evangelists.

With the changes in education over the years since the introduction of the National Curriculum I am aware of the increase in pressure on teachers and head teachers to fulfil the criteria asked of the profession in the changes. I am also aware of the government guidelines with regard to school assemblies and accountability to the Education Authorities about assemblies. There is and will continue to be disagreements amongst teachers and head teachers about the nature of the assembly i.e. the 'Christian content'. The 1944 Education Act has been superceded by the 1988 E.R.A. which states that 'There should be a daily act of worship which is broadly Christian in character.' How this is interpreted is up to the head teacher. But puppet shows in assemblies can be one solution to this area of conflict, a meeting place of church and school with both sides achieving their 'hidden agenda'. And the children benefiting enormously in the process. Here is 'good news' for all!

TO CLERGY: A PERSONAL NOTE

Many clergy are not naturally gifted with children and the prospect of a school assembly may awaken feelings of inadequacy. The safe thing to do is to tell the children a story about a saint, or even preach a diluted sermon. Add to this the not uncommon 'hidden agenda' that really this work in schools should lead to some kind of church visit for the children and there is a recipe for the kinds of disasters many heads have told me about. To sum up all I have heard in one imaginary clergyman we shall call Rev. Outsider: he always tells a story which is above the children's understanding. He expects us to come to his church and says so. He has no idea of the constraints of time in the school day. He doesn't work with us, he does an assembly to us. He feels it's his duty or right to come into the school. He makes the church seem boring.

This kind of thing is happening simply because the clergy are like everyone else – overworked and under-resourced. Do not feel disillusioned about this if you are a clergyman or woman. I hope and pray that as you read on you will be encouraged to have a go with the puppets and know the great joy of making a real impact on your school, or be encouraged to try visiting perhaps for the first time.

When you visit a head teacher, even if the school is in your parish, you can't assume that you will be welcomed with cups of tea and enthusiasm by all. You need to earn your head teacher's respect. I am always aware of this and my approach is respectful and, in short, humble. I arrange an appointment with the head who I am aware has a lot of other things to do and who may not want to see me for a variety of reasons.

1. The head may not be a Christian. I have only met one to date who is.
2. The head does not want to be told what to do in his/her school. The head may feel you represent judgement from the Church.
3. The head has his/her assemblies planned for the term. Are you going to challenge these plans or demand changes?

I say plainly I want to have contact with the school and I want to offer myself to help with assemblies. I will fit in with what has been planned by the head, and perhaps there is a theme we can work on together. Explain that you would like to use puppets as a novel idea in assembly which can also be used as a lead lesson from which Attainment Targets can be realized in the National Curriculum in the form of a short project. The head will want to see what you do and may take up the offer with other members of staff immediately following the show. Or on a long-term basis this could be incorporated at a later stage after a period of planning. A script could be selected as the planned presentation with the appropriate Attainment Targets being highlighted for development. What the head will do is to circulate the script with the ATs to the appropriate members of staff for discussion and possible implementation.

In this way you are offering so much more to the school than an assembly. You will be viewed as perhaps literally a godsend by some. Here is a real way forward for the church and the school to work together for the common good. Amongst the children and staff your 'streetcred' is enhanced. It's up to you to build on that.

TO HEAD TEACHERS

You have a job to do. You have to work within guidelines. The church is here to help you fulfil those guidelines. If you have a clergyman/woman visiting and you like this idea of puppets lend him/her this book. I hope you will try at least one puppet show and develop it to attain the ATs required. You might be familiar with the use of puppets in education. The National Puppet Centre has produced a pack whereby puppets can be used in the National Curriculum. The Attainment Targets are outlined in that pack. I have written resource material to help you in your RE work with appropriate developments in other areas of the curriculum especially in language, technology and art work, and as your staff look at these they will easily produce ideas for learning activities. As an example please read the script of 'Zacchaeus'. Here are some suggested activities to fulfil the ATs.

ZACCHAEUS PUPPET SHOW:
ACTIVITIES TO FULFIL ATTAINMENT TARGETS

English
AT 1 Speaking and listening

Level 1: Participate as speakers and listeners in the presented puppet show. From this, in the classroom, develop the idea of Zacchaeus being small. Talk about short and tall people. Read poems and stories to children about short people. *Snow White and the Seven Dwarfs*, *The Hobbit*, pygmies, *The Water Babies* (Tom became small), *Peter Pan*, *The Borrowers*, an imaginative play about a supermarket – how do you reach the sweets on the top shelf? Asking questions of other shoppers until someone helps.

Level 2: As above with appropriate stories about size. Invent a story about a small person in a group. Perform it as a short play. Discuss the different plays performed with the teacher. With finger puppets and junk puppets direct a play about different-sized people who have an adventure when they meet an important person.

Level 3: Summarize the story of Zacchaeus into a simple message. Tell the story of Zacchaeus in the child's own words, this story to be evaluated for accuracy in small groups. Make a puppet following instructions by the teacher. Use the puppet as a tool to convey a simple message, as say an item of news or general knowledge.

Level 4: Explain clearly the story of Zacchaeus. Talk about taxes. Why did Zacchaeus climb a tree? Why did the people dislike him? Talk about personal likes/dislikes. Interview another child about these personal likes/dislikes and tape-record the interview. Present a puppet play about someone who is disliked.

Level 5: Give a sustained account of a time when a child felt disliked and explain how it felt. Talk about prejudice and justify the point of view. Present a puppet play about prejudice (racial, using different coloured puppets). Talk about variations in vocabulary between different regional and social groups. Explain that Zacchaeus was Jewish, yet worked for Romans. Talk about the rights and wrongs of people in other countries working for poor wages, e.g. Third World labourers working for western companies. Tea pickers. (Zacchaeus had a sort of tea with Jesus.) Talk about the fairness of taxes.

At all levels AT 2, 3 can be achieved through reading and writing about puppets, taxes, etc. Also work in spelling can be achieved.

The simple song which is included after the script can be used in the music area of the National Curriculum and children can accompany the song using simple percussion instruments and fulfil AT 1 at levels 1, 2 and 3.

In mathematics at Level 1, AT 4: Shape and space. Puppets can be made and sorted in size. Work can be done on measuring of heights of the class and of trees using a clinometer at higher levels. Data can be recorded e.g. level 4: Handling data.

There is also historical work on the Roman tax system, and discussion on why the people reacted as they did to tax collectors e.g. AT 1, level 2; Knowledge and understanding.

In technology there is practically no end of applications in making and designing of puppets and props.

In such ways much can be achieved in class using the puppet show as a 'lead lesson'. I believe that the puppet show is an excellent beginning to all kinds of valuable work. The practical advantages of puppetry such as ease of involvement, cheapness and ease of presentation make it an attractive choice for many schools.

Finally I believe this is a wonderful way for the church and the school to work together positively for the benefit of the children, the teachers, and the church's duty to teach the Christian faith. Links between the church and the school can be significantly strengthened which is good news for the wider community which the school and the church are bound to serve. As a Christian I believe this will be a real help to many in their own understanding of the faith, and I believe God will be glorified in our schools through this cooperation.

Reconciliation

In conclusion, after all we have thought about during the course of this book, can we draw our thoughts together into some kind of vision for the use of puppetry in and out of the church? I believe there is a need for this now, or we may begin to think of ourselves as showmen, or that we are entertaining churchpeople. We shall be doing these things in some people's eyes but there is so much more, which I hope you have grasped through the book.

I draw out from the work four main themes which recur in different ways. We shall briefly look at these before drawing a conclusion:

1. INVOLVEMENT

Again and again puppets allow for involvement. This happens in the church and in the wider community when we present the shows. Puppets are one means by which we express our creativity which is God-given. It is a way in which we welcome others in and there are no prominent personalities as the puppets are the personalities. Everyone can take part at a level at which they feel comfortable. Many skills can be used to help in the production of a puppet play and these are to be valued.

2. UNITY

The puppet show unites people in a shared aesthetic experience. It unites them in the presentation of a message. It crosses the boundaries of Christian denomination, age and racial divisions. It also unites people at deeper levels in being able to build a sense of community which shares an experience and is able to laugh together. It helps to break down the isolation many feel in today's world.

3. OUTREACH

Because of the acceptance of puppetry in society puppets are an effective means of outreach for the church into the community at many levels. Because of the involving, unifying effect of puppetry this means of outreach can be entered into by a wide range of Christians. Puppets are a way of communicating the Christian story to young and old and are acceptable to a broad cross section of the community, being accepted at different levels of understanding. Puppets are a point of contact between the church and the wider community.

4. COOPERATION

Puppets are used in the field of education to communicate ideas and values at a non-formal level. They are a point of meeting of church and school and can be used to realize the Attainment Targets of the National Curriculum. In this way there is real cooperation between church and school in the community which is of great benefit to all.

CONCLUSION:
PUPPETS ARE TOOLS FOR RECONCILIATION

Reconciliation is the state of affairs which exists when two or more parties which were in a condition of isolation are brought together and a relationship of peace exists between them. This word is used in the Bible to describe the state of affairs which exists between the believer and God when the barrier which formerly prevented intimate relationship, i.e. sin, has been broken down. This was achieved for us through God sending His son Jesus Christ to die for our sins on a cross. A Christian is a person who has been reconciled with God through accepting the reconciliation offered in Christ. It involved repentance, a turning of the whole person to Christ. The Christian life is then lived in the knowledge and light of reconciliation.

The Christian is urged to live out reconciliation in the world, to seek reconciliation with others, to be an agent of reconciliation. This is taught repeatedly in the New Testament: Jesus taught that the peacemakers were blessed (Matthew 5:9) and His whole life was reconciliation in action. Paul teaches about relationships when he says Christians have a ministry of reconciliation (2 Corinthians 5:18), and makes the statement that all things in heaven and earth are reconciled through Christ (Colossians 1:20). There is then every precedent for believing that 'all things' are the things we should be seeking to find reconciliation in, indeed looking at the coming and goings of human existence and finding where reconciliation is being worked out. To put it another way, to see what God is doing and joining in.

The evidence of my eyes and the testimony of the people I have met whilst being engaged in puppetry lead me to believe that puppets are being used as tools for reconciliation of God's people. Within the church they are another meeting place of denominations and viewpoints. They are another point of contact which brings healing of broken relationships. Out of the church setting they are a meeting place of those who know and those who don't know Christ as Lord. As an activity a puppet show gathers people together in a meaningful experience.

I am committed to work with puppets fundamentally because I am as a Christian committed to working for reconciliation. As you work with your puppets in your own way my prayer is that you will find reconciliation to be the fruit of your practice and performance.

▼▲▼▲▼▲▼▲▼▲▼▲▼▲▼▲▼▲▼▲▼▲▼▲

PART TWO

▼▲▼▲▼▲▼▲▼▲▼▲▼▲▼▲▼▲▼▲▼▲▼▲

Scripts and songs for use

▼▲

Method

The method I use is in fact a very old way of teaching by rhyme, rhythm and repetition. The combination of these three elements makes the show more memorable. The presentation is basically the same in each case, and where special instructions are needed I have indicated this at the beginning of the script. I have also included some simple diagrams so you can easily see where I think the puppets should be positioned. If you have better ideas then of course use them with regard to positioning.

For each script you will need puppeteers, preferably some scenery made from card or artist's foam board, and a puppet theatre – its design is included later in the book. If you haven't yet got a theatre then you can improvise with a table or a sheet draped over a length of rope. The method of presentation is to have a narrator who is between the theatre and the audience. The job of the narrator is to read the script ably and to have the confidence to pause when laughter or drama demand. There is also a small chorus who also have a copy of the script and who recite the lines which are printed in capital letters in the scripts. The audience then repeat the lines which the chorus have recited. In this simple way: 1. The audience are involved in the presentation of the show and enter into the drama. They are kept 'on their toes' as they listen to the story unfold, and their part in it is important. Do stress this before the presentation. 2. The audience are actually repeating parts of the Bible and are so learning Scripture by repetition. If you look at the parts which are repeated, they do communicate salient parts of the story. I have tested children after presentations, and have found a good level of retention immediately after the story. It is this combination of seeing and repeating which doubly reinforces learning.

This then is the basic method I employ with some variation as scripts do require some variety in approach. These parables can be used on their own or as part of a larger presentation, as an introduction to a talk or prayers. The puppeteers are briefly instructed before the show about the simple moves they will make. They gain confidence as they go on. A common mistake to correct is when smaller children do not hold the puppet high enough and it appears half size. Either stop the show and correct it then, or do the show a second time after correcting at the end of the first show. The audience will not condemn this.

I have divided the scripts into four sections: Parables, Furry Friend Talks, Bible Stories Which Are Not Parables, and Raps. I hope this will help you more quickly to find the type of puppet show you are looking for.

Parables

A parable was used by Jesus whenever He wanted to teach. It seems Jesus had an unlimited stock of these, and He drew from people's experience of life. The parables still speak so clearly today. In presenting them as puppet shows I have in no way tried to distract from what we believe Jesus was saying for the sake of effect, for example. Where the scripts rhyme they have adhered as much as possible to the biblical text. Also where the audience repeats lines these are taken from the Bible story.

In this parable of the grain of wheat, reported in John 12:24, Jesus is talking about His death.

A simple seed puppet was made out of a sock, with stick-on eyes and a mouth. We also made a large wheat plant out of a bamboo stick, the head of which was made out of card. Behind the head of the plant we concealed a small box filled with paper seeds. A piece of cotton was attached to the box and at the appropriate moment the cotton was pulled and the seeds cascaded down to the delight of the audience of small children sitting on the floor close by.

SEEDS

A grain of wheat remains a single grain.
Unless it dies and grows again.
Through the cold dark months quite forgotten.
It lies underground amongst things so rotten.
In the darkness of the earth.

God brings new life to birth,
The seed coat splits, out pops a shoot,
A tiny stem a tiny root. (*Animated by fingers in sock*)
The root grows down where water runs,
The stem reaches to the sun,
Until one day quite by surprise,
A small green plant begins to rise.
(*Music during which the plant rises slowly, the seed
   disappears*)
It grows up high into the air,
It grows some leaves and flowers there.
And then more seeds begin to grow,
They fall onto the ground below (*Seeds fall*)
A grain of wheat remains a single grain,
Unless it dies and grows again.

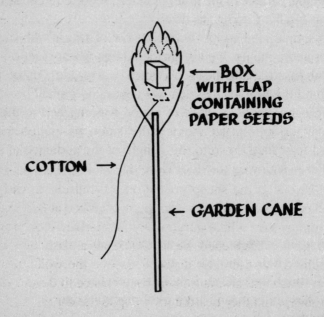

← BOX
WITH FLAP
CONTAINING
PAPER SEEDS

COTTON →

← GARDEN CANE

THE LOST SHEEP

Here is the story of the lost sheep. This one can be acted out in various ways. I use some cuddly toys for this: a lamb, a wolf, and a glove puppet for the shepherd. More audience participation can be enjoyed if you get a group of children to be the bush in which our lamb becomes entangled. This is most effective and the children can hold up bits of coloured paper representing flowers which attract the lamb away from the flock. The action takes place over a wide area, and this script serves as an example of how other stories can be performed. Again a narrator tells the story. The story can be found in Luke 15 and Matthew 18.

Barbara the lamb lived with her mum and dad on the hills overlooking the town of Nazareth. Barbara's mum and dad taught her the things she needed to know. How to keep still when Simon the shepherd cut her fleece. How to keep an eye on her shepherd at all times. How to bleat to let everyone know how she felt. There was the happy bleat, the cross bleat and the frightened bleat (demonstrate these).

Barbara spent most of her life bleating happily and eating the juicy grass which grew on the hillsides. Barbara always did what her parents said and always kept her eye on Simon the shepherd. As long as Simon could be seen, Barbara felt safe.

One day as the sheep grazed on the hillside, a wild lone wolf crept closer and closer to them. It looked at Barbara, and its tummy gave a little gurgling sound. Barbara looked round and gave a frightened bleat. Quick as a flash Simon the shepherd was there, he threw a stone at the wolf and it ran away. But it was always looking for a chance to devour one of the sheep, and they heard it growling in the dark.

Barbara was the youngest of the one hundred sheep in the

flock; her parents always reminded her to keep close to the rest of the flock and never to take her eyes off her shepherd. As long as she remembered this she was happy, but then something terrible happened.

Barbara was muching her juicy grass one day when she smelt a lovely smell, a sweet fragrance that made her mouth water and tummy rumble. She sniffed and sniffed again, and like many sheep who know just a little about life she followed her nose which led her away from the flock and the watchful eye of her shepherd. She wandered off into a strange valley, and there she spied a beautiful bush with wonderful yellow flowers. She sniffed and walked right into the bush. Sharp prickles caught her woolly coat and then she had a little panic, and before long she was quite stuck. She bleated her frightened bleat.

The wolf was sitting in the sun thinking about recipes when he heard one advertising itself 'Lamb in the bush', so off he went to eat his lunch.

The shepherd was doing his evening count of sheep which always sent him off nicely to sleep, '95, 96, 97, 99 . . .' Where was Barbara? Quick as a flash he ran off to look for her. He climbed to the top of the hill and listened. He saw the wolf and picking up a large stone he put it in his sling. The stone hit the wolf on the nose, and off he ran, a stoned lone wolf. Simon gently untangled Barbara from the thorny bush and carried her home singing a happy song.

(Finish with song 'I will search for my sheep'.)

A NON-BIBLICAL PARABLE

This script is not biblical but it can be used as a bridge to Christian teaching about new life in Christ.

▼▲

DYING AND RISING

A puppet parable to illustrate new life, suitable for Easter.

Materials: Caterpillar puppet, stuffed brown sock, card
butterfly, brown paper bag.

Talk: Narrator reads script, puppeteers work puppets.

Being a caterpillar is strange,
It can't always be one, it has to change.
It may like its hairy tum,
And lazing about in the sun.
It may like hanging around,
From a thread above the ground.
It may like crawling on trees,
Or waving its bottom in the breeze.
It may like leaves that are green
And spending its life trying not to be seen.
Munching and crunching every day
Eating cabbages and lettuce away,
Not having to think about tomorrow,
All it does is grow and grow.
But one day very soon,
It's going to be in a cocoon.
Along with all its caterpillar mates,
It will start to naturally pupate.
Its softness will turn to . . . hardness (*pupa appears, i.e.
   paper bag or sock*)
Dull and brown hard and round,
It will hang above the ground.
God intended this to be,
It has to change to be really free.

To become a beautiful butterfly,
The caterpillar has to . . . die.
(*a short piece of music during which the butterfly appears*)

Hi!
I'm a butterfly.
Such a change,
At first I felt strange.
Oi!
What joy,
I didn't think I could be
So beautiful you see.
The old life was all right,
But I was blind now I see the light.
I suppose you'd think I was playing a game
If I told you I'd died and come back again.
But that's how it is with butterflies,
You have to die before you can rise.

THE GOOD SAMARITAN

I suppose I must particularly like this story as it is the first
Bible story I can remember being told. I have written two
scripts for it. One is particularly apt for a church where there is
a degree of self-righteousness. I hope you will find these
helpful and challenging. The method is as usual with the
action coming fast and furious as the robbers set on our
traveller using clubs made of drinking straws. Let the
puppeteers get carried away with this, it's great fun. I usually
perform this without a puppet theatre, but it works just as well
with one even though you will need to be careful to arrange
the puppeteers, as there are seven: two robbers, the traveller, a
priest, a Levite, a Samaritan and an innkeeper.

▼▲▼▲▼▲▼▲▼▲▼▲▼▲▼▲▼▲▼▲▼▲▼▲▼▲▼▲▼▲▼▲▼▲▼▲▼▲

The Good Samaritan I

In the gospel of Luke this story we find,
About a man who wanted to be good and kind.
He wanted to know how to live for ever,
And Jesus said, 'Love God and your neighbour'.
But he persisted, he asked and insisted,
Who his neighbour might be.
So Jesus taught him,
This man who besought Him,
He told him a special story.

With puppets and rhyme, with singing and mime,
We now tell this story to you.
It's Jesus' story we tell,
So please listen well,
And learn some good thing you can do.

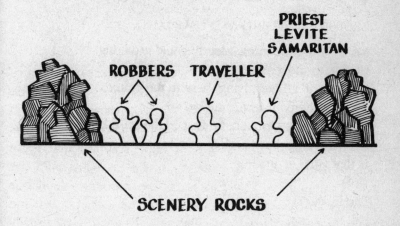

As we begin our puppet show,
A man is travelling to Jericho.
The road he walked was dusty and long,
He felt a little nervous, he may have hummed a little
    song, (*hum*)
For he was on the road all alone,
A long way to go, a long way from home.

A LONG WAY TO GO, A LONG WAY FROM HOME.

Behind a rock some robbers sat,
Waiting for a victim,
Armed with clubs and nasty things like that,
They jumped him, beat him, and stripped him.
He was outnumbered by that cowardly band,
One hit him in the eye, another held his hands.
One hit him on the nose, one bashed him on the head,
They left him in the road, bruised, bleeding, and half-dead.

BRUISED, BLEEDING AND HALF-DEAD.

He lay there moaning, bleeding and groaning,
Unable to move or to cry,
His eyes all aflutter, lying there in the gutter,
And just then a priest came by.
He stopped, he looked, he gasped, he stared,
He walked by on the other side, his nose in the air.
Is that fair?
No!
Did he care?
No!

Then a Levite, (a religious man),
Who worshipped God, who prayed and sang,
Who helped in church, who took the collection,
He came by. What was his reaction?

He stopped, he looked, he gasped, he stared,
He went by on the other side, his nose in the air.
Is that fair?
No!
Did he care?
No!

Then along came another man,
A foreigner, a Samaritan.
With oil and wine he bathed and soothed,
The bleeding cuts that all could see,
He bandaged up every bruise,
And placed him on his donkey.
He took him to the nearest inn,
Asking the landlord to care for him,
And all the bills he promised to pay,
When he'd return another day.
Is that fair?
Yes!
Did he care?
Yes!

So Jesus said to the man who had questioned him,
Who was neighbour to this man?
It was the one who showed mercy to him,
Was it the priest, the Levite, or the Samaritan?

The Good Samaritan 2

A man was on a journey, a long way he had to go,
Travelling a lonely road from Jerusalem to Jericho.
In a lonely rocky place he thought he heard a noise,
And suddenly and brutally he was pounced on by 'the boys'.
They bruised him and they beat him, and kicked him in
   the head,

They stripped him to his birthday suit and left him there half-dead.

WHO WILL HELP HIM, WHO WILL SAVE HIM, WHO WILL SHOW SOME MERCY TO HIM?

Well just by chance as luck would have it a priest came passing by,
He saw that man lying there in the road, he heard him moan and cry.
But the priest was in a hurry, there were people to address,
He had to pray and preach to them, he had a lot to bless.
His sermon couldn't help this man, so he crossed and walked away.
What a nasty interruption to his thoughts this was today.

HE WOULDN'T HELP HIM, HE WOULDN'T SAVE HIM, WHO WILL SHOW SOME MERCY TO HIM?

Well by chance as luck would have it, a Levite came along,
He was thinking godly thoughts, he was humming a godly song. (*hum*)
He thought he did his duty which was set out in God's word,
He knew all about the churches and singing to the Lord.
He saw the man, the victim, lying naked and alone,
He thought he'd read a law about this but his Bible was at home.
So he too ignored him, crossed and walked away.
What a nasty interruption to his worship song today. (*sings*)

HE WOULDN'T HELP HIM, HE WOULDN'T SAVE HIM, WHO WILL SHOW SOME MERCY TO HIM?

So who will come and help our bleeding, dying man?
Not the priest or Levite, but a foreign Samaritan.
He dresses his wounds with oil and wine and takes him
　　to an inn,
And even pays the innkeeper to look after him.
His care for his neighbour showed practical concern.
It is showing mercy to our neighbour that we have to
　　learn.

LAZARUS AND DIVES

In this story which Jesus told we can make much of the
wonderful imagery we are told of. It is easy to make a large
golden heaven with Abraham and Lazarus looking down. This
is best performed by a number of narrators each taking a
different part, as there is quite a lot of dialogue. The story is

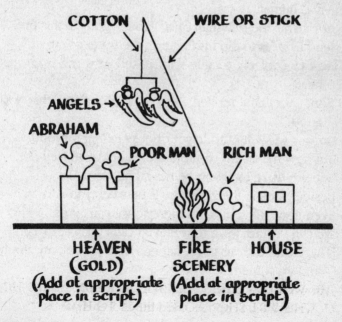

found in Luke 16. You can make simple angels out of card and suspend them from a stick using cotton.

Here is a rich man dressed so well in purple and fine
   linen,
When he dies will he go to Hell or go to God in heaven?
Here's Lazarus, a poor man, for ever begging at the gate
Of the rich man's house. Dogs lick his sores, he's in a
   sorry state.
Weak and poor, covered in sores, Lazarus eventually dies,
Here are the Angels who carry him off to be at Abraham's
   side.
To the rich man who is so well fed, death also comes one
   day,
He is buried and goes to Hell and sees Lazarus far away.
Hell is a place which is terribly hot, the flames get higher
   and higher,
'Abraham,' the rich man calls, 'I'm in agony in this fire.
Send Lazarus to dip his finger in the water so sweet.
He can cool my tongue with it and save me from this
   heat.'
'Son,' Abraham replied, 'you had everything that was
   good,
Lazarus was left outside your house to beg for food.
But now he has his comfort and you have all Hell fire.
You are there in agony, he has all his desires.
Besides look at the gap there is between you and us,
Even if we wanted to, it's there so we can't cross.
We can't come down to Hell, you can't get to heaven.'
'Then send Lazarus to my father's house to see my family
   and warn them.'
'They have the Bible stories to make it all so plain,
Moses and the prophets warn them of this pain.'

'But if someone came back from the grave they would repent instead.'

'If they won't believe the Bible they won't believe if someone rises from the dead.'

THE PHARISEE AND THE PUBLICAN

In the story of the Pharisee and the publican great effect can be obtained by using puppets. The publican can visually tremble and the Pharisee can stand up tall and proud. One or two narrators can be used.

Look at me,
I'm a Pharisee,
My calling is prestigious.
I come to this temple every day,
I stand up here in full view to pray,
I'm ever so religious.
I am better than other men,
Who are such terrible sinners,
I tithe a tenth of all I get,
Twice a week I don't eat two dinners.

Merciful God don't look at me,
I'm a tax collector you see,
And in this temple Lord I pray,
Have mercy on me a sinner today.

Jesus told this story to show that we shouldn't be proud,
We shouldn't want everyone to know that we can pray out
    loud.
It's the humble ones whose prayers are accepted by the
    Lord,
Not the ones who stand up and speak self-exalting words.

FAIRGROUND DISTRACTION

This script was written for a large open-air service to mark the end of the fair in town. It is a spectacle with very large cut-out fairground machine characters. It has subtleties as it was aimed at an adult audience. The cross appears at the end of the show and after concentrating on the fun of the fair appears as an offence. This puppet show would be classified as simple automata and follows a long tradition.

Materials: Large Dodgem, Ferris wheel, roller coaster and merry-go-round characters. A large cross.

Here's Dennis, he's a Dodgem car,
And he spends every day
Thinking he's a Dodgem star,
Beep beep get out of the way.
I'll bash you if you don't move,
I'll spin you round and round,
I've got such a lot to prove,
I can stand my ground.
So many people get in my way,
I'll make them all retreat,
I want to be the best today,
I'll bump everyone I meet.
Broom broom beep beep,
Broom broom beep beep.

Here's Walter, he's a fairground wheel,
And he goes round and round,
Making everyone feel ill,
High above the ground.
Once he starts you're stuck in the air,
Until he lets you down,

He really doesn't seem to care,
He thinks he's the talk of the town.
He's never got anything new to say,
He hasn't got any fears,
He's always going the same way,
He never hears new ideas.
Round and round.
Round and round.

Here's Roger, he's a roller coaster,
He's never gone off the rails,
Of all the rides he is a boaster,
His pride it never fails.
He's never wandered on the bends,
He's dipped and climbed so high,
And all day long his time he spends
Climbing to the sky.
He'd really like to leave his tracks,
But he's never found the tool,
To help him get his freedom back,
He only knows the rules.
Click clack
Click clack.

Marion is a merry-go-round,
Everything is bright,
Always making happy sounds,
Everything's all right.
Worry never comes near her,
She doesn't want to know,
She isn't at all a carer,
Life's a carousel, all go!
You can spend all day with her,
Trying too not to care,

Never a tear you'll shed with her,
Never a prayer you'll share.
Smile smile,
Smile smile.

Life can seem like a funfair with all its different rides,
Life is made of ups and downs and from it you can hide.
People all have problems and however hard they try,
They can't hide all their weakness, sometimes people cry.
For God made human beings to find true joy in Him,
And what we're used to seeing is people lost in sin.
The fair can't last for ever, you have to leave the fun,
But Jesus is with you always when once your heart He's
    won.
He'll help you be unselfish, He'll pull you off your track,
To follow Him as Lord and King there'll be no going
    back.
The cross isn't attractive in fact it isn't fair
That God's own Son should bear our sins in such agony
    there.

Man makes machines which give passing fun; he also
    made the cross,
Which crucified God's only Son who gave His life for us.
Whenever we look at the cross we remember Jesus died,
We can't pretend that life is fine when we see Jesus
    crucified.
So we'll leave behind the funfair, we'll look to the cross
    instead,
And repent of all our sins today for which our Saviour
    bled.
Can we ever be truly happy with the world's idea of fun,
When we think of all we'd rather do than look to God's
    dear Son?

Furry friend talks

Here are a selection of talks you can use with a larger hand-held puppet. The skills involved in the successful performance of these scripts are to be revised from chapter 7. These can also be performed with soft toys if you don't have a puppet.

SHY AND FRIGHTENED

Aim: To introduce a puppet character to a group, and in so doing to teach that God is with us when we feel lonely.

Presentation: Before you begin to talk, 'plant' these objects on three children.
A piece of food (chocolate biscuit?)
A small toy
A Bible.

Talk outline: In the box I have a special friend I'd like you to meet. The problem is he is very shy and frightened. Has anyone here been shy and frightened? (Find out when and why) What can we do to help those who are new? (Three answers to pick up on: sharing food, toys and stories to cheer the person up.) As the answers come out call your helpers out one by one to give their gift to your puppet. As the last one brings out the story book explain it is a very special book. The book is special because it is God's Word, it teaches us that God loves us and the Lord Jesus is waiting for us to talk to Him. (Go

on to tell how lots of people have found a friend in Jesus, close
with a prayer.)

SONGS: 'When I needed a neighbour'
        'One more step along the world I go'
        'Wide wide as the ocean'

What this script achieves in a very short time is a rapport with
the children which you can later build upon.

A TALK FOR BIBLE SUNDAY

Aim: To teach that God speaks to us through the Bible.

Materials: Sunbed goggles, magnifying glass, two pairs of
cardboard spectacles coloured red and blue to fit puppet.

Presentation: As you talk you place the various materials
one by one over the puppet's eyes. Enlist a helper to hold the
Bible, or put it on a lectern.

Talk outline: Today we are going to talk about reading our
Bibles and as usual I have my friend to help me. Can you read?
(Puppet shakes its head.) The first way we hear about God is
through people telling us. They too have heard Bible stories
from their parents or teachers, or a minister or priest, or they
may even have read them for themselves. The trouble is we
read the Bible in so many different ways. Let me show you all
how that happens with the help of my friend here.

1. (Put red specs on puppet.) Some people tend always to
look on the bright side of life, some think that being a
Christian is all happiness and fun. They may tell this to
others. They look at the Christian life through 'rose-

coloured spectacles'. The Bible has a lot to say about happiness, but it also speaks about sad things, and Jesus suffered a great deal. (Take off specs.)

2. (Put blue specs on puppet.) Some people tend to look on the blue side of life, and find consolation in the sadder parts of the Bible. This is fine if we are feeling sad, but we can become a bit narrow-minded if that's all we read. Our Bible reading needs to be balanced; following Bible notes helps to keep a balance between happy and sad passages. (Take specs off.)

3. (Use magnifying glass.) Some people take one little verse of the Bible and magnify it to give it a meaning that isn't right. We must see the Bible as a whole and not take little bits out of context. This is how people form sects.

4. (Use sunbed goggles.) Some people seem to filter the Bible. They look at it simply as they would look at any other book, filtering out the work of the Holy Spirit. Christians believe that the Bible is a special book which God Himself inspired.

Conclusion: When we come to read the Bible, we need to read lots of different parts of it. As we do this we can pray that God will speak to us through its pages, that He will open our eyes to see Jesus, and guide us to a balanced Christian life, so we can grow up to know so much more about God.

A TALK FOR MOTHERING SUNDAY

Aim: To teach about salvation.

Materials: Puppet, a posy of flowers made from a rose, some greenery, and a daffodil.

Mothering Sunday is an opportunity to tell the Christian story to those who perhaps do not usually come to church. The puppet here is used to teach, and your story is presented to the audience with the additional visual aid of the posy of flowers. The combination of the puppet and the posy captures the attention of a wide age-range, and if you present a posy to all the mums they hopefully will remember at home what was taught in church.

Presentation: Talk about how your puppet character was out early in the morning and could only find these three plants to make a posy with. After some chat say that this is indeed a posy with possibilities for as we're in church we can learn more about Jesus from it. For the posy reminds you of three things from the Bible.

1. A Posy of Proof: Look at the greenery, isn't it beautiful? Just by looking around us we can see the beautiful world that God has made. St Paul in his letter to the Romans reminds us in chapter 1, v.20–21 that ever since the world was made God's eternal power and divine nature can be clearly seen through what He has made. But mankind disregarded this proof of God's existence and refused to thank Him. Being thankless is bad, isn't it?

2. A Posy of Pardon: Look at this thorny rose you have picked. Because of man's thanklessness to God, because of his disobedience in the Garden of Eden we hear in the Bible in Genesis chapter 3 that all of creation becomes flawed. Women would have trouble in pregnancy and the earth would have to be cleared of thorns before we could plant food. This was part of God's judgement. (You can illustrate this with appropriate examples.) But God is merciful and He loves us. He sent His Son who lived a sinless life and

died for us on a cross. Through His death things are put right and at His crucifixion they placed a crown of thorns on His head. We and all of creation are put right with God through the Lord Jesus Christ's sacrifice.

3. A Posy of Promise: Here you've picked a daffodil. Every year it lies in the ground but it blooms again. Jesus died and they buried Him, but after three days He rose again. He gives us the promise of eternal life if we repent and believe in Him. The golden daffodil reminds us of God's promise to us of new life.

Follow the maker's instructions

Materials: Puppet, car manual.

Presentation: Only the other day I was driving down the road in my car when in my rear-view mirror I saw Higgins jumping up and down on the back seat. 'Boing boing' he went. I was taking him to a party and I got rather cross. Why do you think I got cross? (Children answer, tease out idea that it is dangerous and against the law to travel without a seat belt.) There you are, Higgins, I told you so, but you wouldn't believe me. Perhaps you'll believe them? (Puppet shakes its head.) Well, if you won't believe me and you won't believe them perhaps you'll believe this. (Open your car manual and 'read') 'Seat belts are to be worn at all times when travelling in the car; for safety follow the manufacturer's instructions.'

God has given us instructions to live by, they are there for our safety and they are found in His 'Maker's instructions', the Bible. Let's look at them, they are called God's Law. (Read the Ten Commandments, or Jesus' summary of the Law.)

A TALK FOR USE WITH A CHRISTINGLE

Aim: To teach that Jesus is the light of the world.

Presentation: You will need a Christingle. For the candle use a joke birthday candle, one which relights once it has been blown out.

Light the candle and hold the Christingle in one hand, work

the puppet with the other hand. Allow the candle to burn as you tell the audience about the meaning of the different parts of the Christingle. Last of all tell about the candle representing Jesus the light of the world. As you say this open the puppet's mouth, and with the candle close to your mouth blow it out. Tell your puppet off about this bad behaviour in the middle of your talk. As the candle relights make as though you haven't seen it and the puppet has. (i.e. you are appearing to look at the puppet.) Children will let you know it has relit. You can make the puppet blow it out again; of course it relights.

Make the point nothing can put out the light of Jesus in the world, and give examples.

Songs: 'The light of Christ has come into the world'
'Colours of day'

GOD COMES TO US

This talk is particularly suitable for Advent or Christmas.

Materials: Two puppets or soft toys.

Presentation: Ask for two volunteers to hold characters and to be an aeroplane! As you tell the story stand amongst the audience facing the two at the front so you can encourage them in the actions. To begin, arrange your two helpers thus . . .

Story: One day Teddy Pilot decided to take Robert Rabbit for a fly about in his aeroplane. They started the engine (children make noise) and zoomed up into the sky (helpers lean back). They banked to the left (use your arms, helpers will copy), they banked to the right, they zoomed higher, then lower. Then they looped the loop (much hilarity as the helpers attempt this). Robert was feeling sick. Teddy turned to him and said, 'ISN'T IT GOOD TO BE HERE? UP HERE WE'RE CLOSER TO GOD.' (Get one of your helpers to repeat this.)

Ask the children. 'Do you agree, are you nearer to God up in an aeroplane?' After discussion read them the prologue to John's Gospel and explain how God comes to us in Jesus.

Songs: 'Emmanuel'
       'Lord Jesus Christ'

Bible stories which are not parables

ZACCHAEUS

This story is very effective especially if a large cut-out tree is used for Zacchaeus to 'leg up' and is positioned at one side of the play area. A cut-out house is placed at the other end. By doing this the characters enter and exit from fixed points and do not just pop up. This is best performed by three puppeteers, one as Jesus, one as two of the crowd and one as Zacchaeus. Again a narrator and a small chorus are used. The story is found in Luke 19.

Tree with hole for puppets head

Zacchaeus   Jesus   House

Onlookers
slightly behind.

Zacchaeus is a funny name to the likes of you and me,
He was easy to overlook for he was small you see.
He lived in a very busy town by the name of Jericho,
The story we are about to hear happened long ago.

LONG, LONG AGO.

Zacchaeus collected taxes and because he was the boss,
No one really noticed if some of the money was lost.
He wasn't very honest, he used to cheat the folk,
And when you paid him extra that really was no joke.
People didn't like him for those things he used to do,
And when they saw him on the street they would hiss and
    boo.

HISS, BOO!

But Zacchaeus didn't really care, he found it rather funny,
And if the people hated him so what? he had their
    money.
When all was said and done in fact he thought he was a
    winner,
He didn't really seem to know he was a dreadful sinner.

HE WAS A DREADFUL SINNER.

Then one bright and glorious day Jesus came passing
    by.
Zacchaeus had heard of Jesus and he thought that he
    would try
To find this man they talked about, this preacher they
    came to see.
But folks were tall and he was small so he legged it up a
    tree.

HE LEGGED IT UP A TREE.

Peeping from the branches, hiding in the leaves,
He looked down on Jesus hardly daring to breathe.
For he felt strangely guilty about the things he'd done,
Cheating all the people who now crowded in the sun.
He felt so separated from all the folks below,
Well he had seen this Jesus, but now he ought to go,
He'd go and have his dinner as usual all alone,
In his richly furnished and decorated tax-free home.
And just as he was ready to sneak off and run away,
He heard his name 'Zacchaeus get down, I'm coming to
   your house today.'
Before he could think of an excuse he was kneeling in
   the road,
Amazed and rather embarrassed at the stares of the angry
   crowd.
For the people started to mutter, complain and talk
   aloud,
Jesus going with that sinner, it shouldn't be allowed.

IT SHOULDN'T BE ALLOWED.

But much to their amazement he got up from the floor,
And said, 'Look, Lord, here and now I give half my things
   to the poor,
And if I have cheated anyone through fiddling the
   accounts,
I promise I will pay them back four times the amount.'
Zacchaeus he was happy, he didn't count the cost,
And Jesus said, 'Salvation has come to this man who was
   lost.'

SALVATION HAS COME TO THIS MAN WHO WAS LOST.

Zacchaeus climbed the tree that day so he could clearly
   see
Jesus the Son of God who came to set us free.

May we too be in the place clearly to see the Lord,
And turn away from all our sins and listen to His Word.
May our lives clearly show that we follow Him,
Daily living honestly, repenting of our sins.
(There is a song which goes well with this, 'Zacchaeus')

LEVI

Again the tax-collecting theme can be expanded into a service and perhaps the story of Levi also included. I prefer to perform this as a wide puppet show starting at Levi's booth and moving on to Levi's house, where the puppets gather round a large table.

It is equally effective as a show in the theatre but if it is being shown along with Zacchaeus a different method of presentation adds variety. The story is found in Mark 2, Luke 5 and Matthew 9.

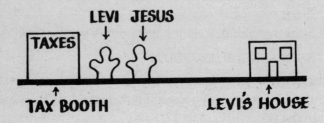

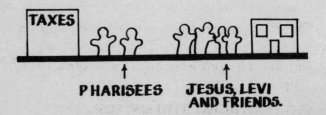

Here's a man called Levi, his job is tax-collecting,
With a bit of fiddling he gets by, I wonder who suspects
him?
A penny here a penny there, added to every bill,
He doesn't seem to have a care, he eats and drinks his
fill.
And at night when he's drunk his wine, and eaten his
finest meat,
He sits alone and spends his time thinking who else he
can cheat.
His friends are also like him, fiddling in every way,
Not really caring that they sin. But Levi will change
today.

LEVI WILL CHANGE TODAY.

For Jesus is coming along the road, and Levi wants to
see,
Jesus walks right up to him and says to him 'Follow me'.

JESUS SAYS TO HIM FOLLOW ME

And without hesitation he leaves his cushy job,
And follows Jesus Christ the Lord, no more to steal and
rob.
And straight away he offers all the things he has,
His life, his home, his coffers, everything he was.
So Jesus goes to Levi's house on this special day,
Levi's friends come from round about, to hear what Jesus
will say.
The Pharisees and teachers come and see Jesus eating
dinner,
And ask the Lord's disciples, 'Why does He eat with
sinners?'

WHY DOES HE EAT WITH SINNERS?

Jesus heard them speaking and saw them looking pious,
'I have come to save sinners,' He said, 'not those who are
   righteous.'
For Jesus came to save everyone, the poor and the
   wealthy.
'It is the sick who need a doctor,' He said, 'not those who
   are healthy.'

IT IS THE SICK WHO NEED A DOCTOR, NOT THOSE
WHO ARE HEALTHY.

So from this Bible story let's learn not to lie and steal,
And following Levi's example we too can share our
   meals.
For it is in giving that we meet our deepest need,
Let's truly follow Jesus in thought and word and deed.

THE STILLING OF THE STORM

Here is yet another method of presentation which relies on
the narrator feeding the puppeteers lines. This is based on an
idea I saw Maggie Durran perform with a few additions by
myself. I like to sit the children round the action pretending to
be the hills around the sea with a gap in one end to show how
the wind funnels up the valley. This story can be found in
Luke 8, Mark 4 and Matthew 8.

Materials: Glove puppets, boat cut out of card. Large sheets
of thick card for thunder effects.

Presentation: Stand your volunteers at the front, each
holding their puppet behind the boat. Jesus is in the rear.

Explain to the audience that you are going to split them into three groups: wind, rain, thunder. Practise their sound effects: wind blows, rain taps fingers on hands, thunder shakes pieces of card and stamps feet.

Talk: As you tell the story get the puppeteers to repeat your lines, individuals taking different parts.

One day Jesus got into a boat with his disciples and said, 'Let's go over to the other side of the lake.' (*Various agreements: yes, good idea, etc.*) So they set off (*singing*). Then Jesus fell asleep. Suddenly a strong wind blew up (*audience blow*), the rain began to fall (*audience tap*), it got harder (*tap harder*). Then it started to thunder (*audience thunder*). The disciples became very frightened (*help, I want my mum, I feel sick, etc.*) and woke Jesus up. 'Save us', they said. Jesus gave a command: 'Be still.' (*All goes quiet.*) Jesus said, 'Why are you frightened, have you no faith?' They all said, 'Who is this man? Even the wind and waves obey Him!'

Songs: 'With Jesus in the boat we can smile at the storm'
         'Be still and know that I am God'

The quiet that comes after all the noise is very dramatic; we have often gone straight into prayer from this point or sung very quietly.

JESUS IN THE TEMPLE

(Luke 2:41–52)

This show involves as many puppets as you like to be the crowds. It is a good idea to use finger puppets for this. I perform this without a puppet theatre. There are two crowds,

one on the journey which Mary and Joseph leave, and another
in the city. The story is told by a narrator and a chorus.

On a long and dusty road Mary and Joseph are walking,
They're going home to Nazareth, thinking, and praying,
    and talking.
They've been up to Jerusalem, the holy city of the Jews,
Celebrating Passover, hearing again the good news
Of how God had delivered Israel from the time when
    they were slaves.
To Pharaoh down in Egypt and how God came to save
The people from oppression at Pharaoh's soldier's hands,
How He led them from slavery to their promised land.

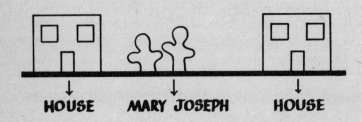

↓	↓	↓
HOUSE	**MARY JOSEPH**	**HOUSE**

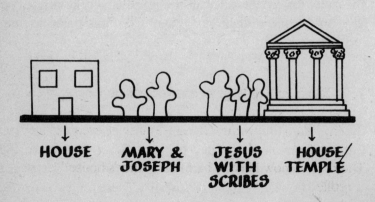

↓	↓	↓	↓
HOUSE	**MARY & JOSEPH**	**JESUS WITH SCRIBES**	**HOUSE/ TEMPLE**

It was such a celebration everyone had to come,
Mary and Joseph had been to the temple with Jesus their
    only son.
And now as they're out of the city, enjoying the fresh air,
They look around for Jesus, but He isn't there.
Mary and Joseph are worried, they look for Him high and
    low,
He isn't with their company so back to Jerusalem they
    must go.

BACK TO JERUSALEM THEY MUST GO.

For three whole days they search for Him in and out of
    places,
But they cannot find Him amongst all the pilgrims' faces,
So at last they come to the temple where they'd been
    some days before,
And Jesus is sitting and questioning the teachers of the
    law.

JESUS IS SITTING AND QUESTIONING THE TEACHERS
    OF THE LAW.

Everyone was listening to what Jesus had to say,
But Mary and Joseph have other things to say to Him
    today.
'Son,' Mary says, 'why have you treated us like this, don't
    you care?
Your father and I have been worried and have been
    searching everywhere.'
But they didn't fully understand His answer even though
    they tried,
'Didn't you know I had to be in my Father's house?' Jesus
    replied.

'DIDN'T YOU KNOW I HAD TO BE IN MY FATHER'S HOUSE?' JESUS REPLIED.

In obedience to His parents Jesus went back home with them,
He grew in wisdom and stature and in favour with God and men.

HE GREW IN WISDOM AND STATURE AND IN FAVOUR WITH GOD AND MEN.

THE TEMPTATIONS

Here is another scene from Christ's life, and it is quite all right to use an ordinary puppet for Satan, but if you can obtain one of the more Red Devil types this will also do. Some shops sell these things to hang in cars. Be adventurous with the scenery and allow for scene changes with some spooky incidental music.

The story of the temptations of Christ can be found in Matthew 4, Mark 1 and Luke 4.

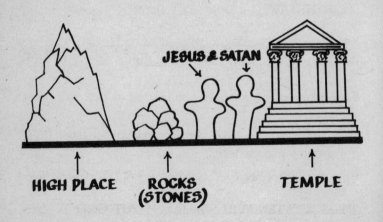

JESUS & SATAN

HIGH PLACE   ROCKS (STONES)   TEMPLE

After Jesus had been baptized by His cousin John,
He was led into the wilderness to be tempted by the evil
  one.
Even the wild animals knew Jesus was the King,
The lions saw the lamb of God but they didn't try to harm
  Him.

THEY DIDN'T TRY TO HARM HIM.

After forty days and forty nights fasting in that place,
The devil came to tempt the Lord, he met Him face to
  face.
This was no chance meeting but all part of God's plan,
Jesus had to be tempted as a weak and hungry man.
'If you are the Son of God command these stones to
  become bread'.
'It is written man shall not live by bread alone but by
  God's Word,' Jesus said.

'MAN SHALL NOT LIVE BY BREAD ALONE BUT BY GOD'S
  WORD', JESUS SAID.

Then the devil took Jesus to the temple in Jerusalem, the
  holy city,
And stood Him on the pinnacle and tried again to tempt
  Him without pity.
'If you are the Son of God why don't you throw yourself
  down?
Angels will come and catch you, you won't strike your
  foot on a stone.'
Jesus wasn't going to do that to prove He was the best.
He replied, 'It is written you shall not put God to the test.'

'IT IS WRITTEN YOU SHALL NOT PUT GOD TO THE
  TEST.'

Satan took Jesus to a high place and showed him lands
and seas.

'All of this I will give you,' Satan said, 'if you will worship
me.'

Jesus wouldn't give Satan what he didn't deserve.

'Go away,' He said. 'God alone is to be worshipped and
served.'

'GOD ALONE IS TO BE WORSHIPPED AND SERVED.'

Satan couldn't tempt Jesus to sin, even though he tried,

He'd done his worst but couldn't win, he'd cheated and
he'd lied.

Then glory came to that wilderness and angels gathered
round,

They looked after Jesus the Son who'd stood His ground.

Jesus was tempted in every way but He didn't sin.

He helps us in our weakness, and with His help we win.

MOSES

In this script you engage the children's attention through the
character of the firefly which is the way of introducing the
burning bush. The firefly is made from a cut-out piece of paper
attractively coloured. It hovers above the children seated on
the ground by means of a piece of cotton. As the story
progresses move over to the puppet theatre and watch the
show.

Materials: Firefly (simple marionette), glove puppet of
Moses, a cut-out burning bush of card covered in shiny red
foil.

'Here's Freddie, he's a firefly,
As if you didn't know,
He hovers and he darts,
His body is aglow.
His wings are brightly coloured,
And look they seem to shine,
He lives out in the desert,
On Mount Horeb in Palestine.

Now with imagination we can see him fly,
We hear his wings are rustling as he goes darting by.
He's looking for his firefly friends,
For an illuminating chat,
But suddenly he stops and stares,
Well, will you look at that!

For over there can you see?
The whole mountain seems to glow,
Is that Freddie's little firefly friends
Meeting down below?

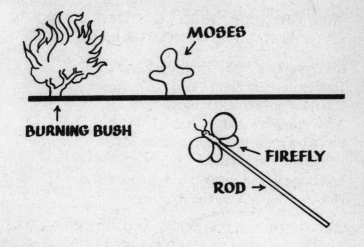

Let's go with Freddie firefly,
And see this strange bright sight
That brightens up the evening,
With such a burning light.

It's a burning bush on the mountain,
What can this be about?
There's a man standing close beside,
Is he trying to put it out?

The man we see is Moses,
God's chosen him for a plan,
The bush is calling out his name,
Moses says, 'Here I am.'

MOSES SAYS, 'HERE I AM'.

God's voice is calling from the bush,
What a strange and powerful sound,
'Take off your shoes,' God says to Moses,
'You're standing on holy ground.'

'TAKE OFF YOUR SHOES,' GOD SAYS TO MOSES,
   'YOU'RE STANDING ON HOLY GROUND.'

God says, 'I have heard my people's cry,
They're slaves in Egypt's land,
You must go and rescue them,
From Pharaoh's soldiers' hands.
You must bring them out of there,
I'll be with you, do not worry,
And bring them to a good and spacious land,
Flowing with milk and honey.'

'BRING THEM TO A GOOD AND SPACIOUS LAND,
   FLOWING WITH MILK AND HONEY.'

But Moses says, 'Who am I that I should save them from
  this king?'
God replies, 'You will worship me on this mountain with
  the people you will bring.'
But Moses says 'What is your name that I can use?'
God replies, 'Tell them I AM sent you and they won't
  refuse.'

'TELL THEM I AM SENT YOU AND THEY WON'T REFUSE.'

Then three miracles God shows to him to help him
  understand:
A snake from a stick, blood from water, and a leprous
  hand.
But Moses protests to God, 'This thing I cannot do.'
God says, 'Your brother Aaron will speak to them and I
  will be with you.'

'YOUR BROTHER AARON WILL SPEAK TO THEM AND I
WILL BE WITH YOU.'

Freddie the firefly was amazed at what he saw that day,
Moses was called by God and listened to what he should
  say.
He tried to excuse himself from all that God required,
But God's voice he heard strong and clear, speaking from
  the fire.
When God asks us to do something we too try to excuse
Ourselves by lots of talking, but we really can't refuse.

JEPHTHAH'S RASH VOW

This story was performed as a show by our puppeteering
forebears; there are recorded scripts from 1701, 1744 and
1749. It was a script I wanted to perform anew. It is acted out
by the puppets with suitable sound effects produced by a

chorus. For props you make a cut-out house and Jephthah's unfortunate daughter appears through a cut-out door. Jephthah wields a sword, and you provide two cut-out armies to stage the battle. On Jephthah's return the army appear on stage with him. Four puppeteers are required: Jephthah, his daughter, two rod puppeteers to be the armies.

Jephthah was a warrior, he led the Israelites;
Long ago he struck a blow against the Ammonites.
The Ammonites were fossilized in their wicked ways,
They did not worship the one true God, idols they would
   praise.

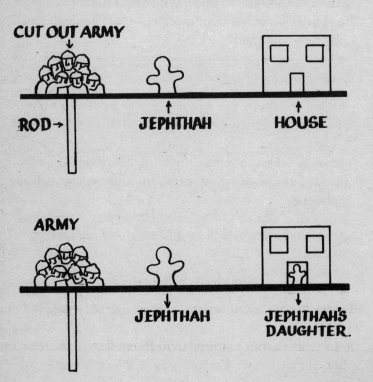

Israel had to capture land promised to them by the Lord,
They marched into battle with spears and clubs and
    swords.
Then Jephthah made a vow to God to ensure he'd win the
    fight:
'If Israel wins the battle and the Ammonites are put to
    flight,
Whoever comes out of my front door to meet me when I
    return,
I will give as sacrifice, an offering I will burn.
An offering I will burn.'

So Jephthah fought the Ammonites and defeated them,
He devastated twenty towns then went back home again.
The Israelites shook tambourines, they praised and
    clapped their hands.
The battle was now over and they possessed the land.
But remember Jephthah's vow to God, the rash one that
    he swore?
Who will come to meet him out of his front door?
Who will come to meet him out of his front door?

The Israelites were rejoicing, the scene was really wild,
And out of Jephthah's front door comes his daughter, his
    only child.

It was then Jephthah remembered the vow he chose to
    make,
He had to sacrifice her and his vow he couldn't break.
'Daughter, oh my daughter, how sad I am today!'
He tore his clothes in misery and listened to what she'd
    say.
He tore his clothes in misery and listened to what she'd
    say.

'Father, oh my father, God you cannot test,
All I ask is you grant me one final request.
I'll roam the hills for two more months and with my
    friends I'll weep.
For I will never marry now, your vow you have to keep.
I will never marry now, your vow you have to keep.'

God made the final sacrifice in Jesus Christ our Lord,
And what He asks of us today is obedience to His
    word.
No rash vows or promises will earn a victory,
Trust in Jesus, God's own Son, now sets God's people
    free.
Trust in Jesus, God's own Son, now sets God's people
    free.

DAVID AND GOLIATH

This story is performed using two large rod puppets cut out of
foam board or card. A polystyrene ball was put on a wire and at
the point in the story where David slays Goliath it flies through
the air. The Goliath puppet has a movable arm attached to the
body with a paper fastener. The audience are split into two
armies to sing and shout at each other. Each army is led by a
cheerleader who has a copy of the script. The narrator reads
the story. The theatre has a hill at each end which the puppets
enter from behind, so they don't pop up.

The Philistines were enemies of the Israelites,
They were always ready and waiting for a fight.
One day they face each other waiting for the kill,
A valley set between them, each army on a hill.

(SHOUTS AND BOOS FROM THE ARMIES)

Goliath was a mighty man of the Philistines, (*enter Goliath*)

He stood over three metres tall on the battle lines.

He wore a heavy suit of armour and a helmet shining bright,

His javelin strapped to his back, what a fearful sight.

If this wasn't quite enough to make you quake with fear,

Look at his mighty muscles, look at the size of his spear!

A soldier went before him carrying his shield,

Goliath stood invincible upon the battlefield.

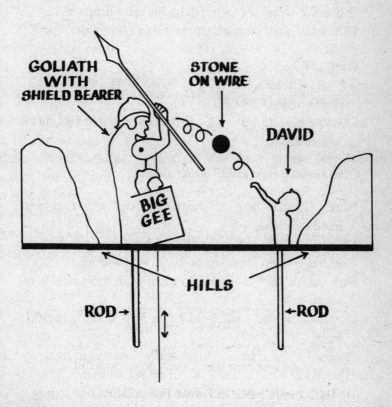

PHILISTINES:
GOLIATH IS OUR CHAMPION HE WORKS OUT IN THE
    GYM,
HE IS BIG AND MUSCULAR. AREN'T YOU SCARED OF
    HIM?

As if this wasn't quite enough to make the soldiers rout,
He opened up his great big mouth and he began to shout,
'Choose a man and send him down here to fight with me,
If I win you'll be our slaves if I lose your servants we'll
    be.'

At this the Israelites were frightened and dismayed,
Who will fight this mighty man who isn't afraid?

ISRAELITES:
WE ARE TREMBLING AT THE KNEES, WE ARE FRIGHT-
    ENED AND DISMAYED,
COMPARED TO HIM WE LOOK LIKE FLEAS! HELP! WE
    ARE AFRAID!

(*Exit Goliath behind hill. Enter David.*)

Here's David, he's a shepherd boy, a strong and
    handsome lad,
He has brothers in the army and Jesse is their dad.
God has chosen David to be Israel's new king,
He's on his way to the camp today with food he's been
    asked to bring.
Down upon the battlefield he sees Goliath, a terrible
    sight,
He goes to Saul, Israel's king, and volunteers to fight.
He will not wear armour, it's of no use to him,
He'll go and fight Goliath with five pebbles and a sling.

ISRAELITES:
DAVID'S GOT A SLING, PEBBLES AND A SLING
EEE AYE ADIO DAVID'S GOT A SLING.

PHILISTINES:
WE'VE GOT A BIG MAN, HIT HIM IF YOU CAN,
EE AYE ADIO WE'VE GOT A BIG MAN.

(*Israelites and Philistines sing at one another.*)

(*Goliath and David face one another.*)

Goliath curses David, he'll feed his flesh to the birds,
Wild beasts will eat his carcass. He shouts his angry
  words.
David says, 'You come at me with spear and javelin,
Today my God will strike you down and with God's help
  I'll win.
The Lord will save His people and not by sword or spear,
There is a God in Israel whom you do not fear.
This day the Lord will hand you over to me and I'll strike
  you down dead,
And then I'll finish off the job by cutting off your head.'
Goliath wasn't happy to hear this awful thing,
He moved towards young David who put a stone in his
  sling.
Quick as a flash the stone was thrown and through the air
  it sped,
It hit Goliath between the eyes and he fell down dead.

(*CHEERS, SHOUTS, WHISTLES*)

Israel was victorious because of David and his sling,
As a man by God's plan he was crowned as Israel's king.

RAPS

Rapping is a lot of fun, and this way of telling the Bible stories seems to have particular appeal to younger teenagers. The best method is to have the whole thing taped with a backing rhythm. I use a rabbit puppet for these raps, who mouths in time with the tape. If you have a script at hand it is easy to do. You should have a group as the chorus, and the audience repeats what they say in time with the rap. Make sure that you leave a space on your tape for this to happen. I call my puppet 'Roger Rap-it'. In addition you can act out the drama with hand puppets, rod puppets, or marionettes. Have fun.

THE ANDREW RAP

John's gospel 1:35—42

John the Baptist preached the news,
'bout Jesus Christ to all the Jews.
Some folk came and listened to him,
And believed his words 'bout peoples' sin.

THEY BELIEVED HIS WORDS 'BOUT PEOPLE'S SIN.

One of the Jews that John knew,
Was a Galilean fisherman called Andrew.
One day with a friend he was listening to John,
When Jesus Christ came walking along.

JESUS CHRIST CAME WALKING ALONG.

John saw Jesus, he knew He was the Lord,
He said, 'Look! there is the Lamb of God.

JOHN SAID, 'LOOK! THERE IS THE LAMB OF GOD.'

'Rabbi,' they asked Him, 'Where are you livin'?'
'Come and see,' Jesus said, so they went with Him.
They went to a place and they talked all day,
They heard what Jesus had to say.
Andrew fetched Peter his brother,
He said, 'We have found the Messiah.'

HE SAID, 'WE HAVE FOUND THE MESSIAH.'

So Andrew was a disciple of John,
He followed Jesus, God's own Son.
He told his brother Peter to come and see,
He was the original missionary.

WE DON'T SEE WHY WAS HE
A MISSIONARY?

A missionary is someone who,
Tells folk about Jesus,
So how about you?
If you've got a brother, a sister or a mother,
A father or a daughter, son, husband or wife,
Tell about Jesus, God's Son, our Saviour,
And the hope of eternal life.

GETHSEMANE

Presentation: Disciple glove puppets act out story. Narrator
or others perform rap.

I've a story to tell so listen to me,
It's about a garden called Gethsemane.

Say it to me, Gethsemane.

GETHSEMANE

Say it so I hear it,
Gethsemane.

GETHSEMANE

This story happened long ago,
It's a story you should know.
It's about a man called Jesus,
God's own Son,
How He was left all alone
In that garden late at night,
And He didn't want to fight.
For evil men were after Him,
Even though He'd done nothin'
That was wrong or mad or cruel or bad,
He was kind and gentle but very sad.
Alone in the garden He felt so weak,
All His friends had fallen asleep.
Lemme hear you speak,
They'd fallen asleep.

THEY'D FALLEN ASLEEP.

Say it so I hear it,
They'd fallen asleep.

THEY'D FALLEN ASLEEP.

He knew in His heart He'd be rejected,
And very soon He'd be arrested.
They would come to take Him away
And while He waited He knelt and prayed.
He fell on the ground down in the mud,

And the sweat on His brow was like drops of blood.
To God His Father He pleaded and cried,
For He knew He would be crucified.
Gimme that line,
He'd be crucified.

HE'D BE CRUCIFIED.

Say it so I hear it,
He'd be crucified.

HE'D BE CRUCIFIED.

This story I'm telling now gets worse,
A man called Judas who had a purse,
With money that they gave him,
To betray Him
Came and kissed Him,
So they seized Him.
They took Him away with clubs and swords,
The King of kings and Lord of lords
Was left without a friend to save Him.
God so loved us that He gave Him
Into the hands of sinful men,
So we could be born again.
On a cross in our place
He took all the sad disgrace.
We deserved the death He died,
We have cheated, stolen and lied.
But He took the punishment for our sin,
He saw it through, He didn't give in.
He was arrested in Gethsemane;
Say it with me, Gethsemane.

GETHSEMANE.

Say it so I hear it, Gethsemane.

GETHSEMANE.

WAITING

This rap was written for a diocesan youth camp and is based
on Ecclesiastes 3.

Life ain't easy it's plain to see,
Things don't come to us easily.
You have to work to get your pay,
To buy the things you need each day.
Pocket money how much do you need?
If you want a lot it has to be greed.
You might want to stay up late,
But to stay up late you have to wait.

YOU GOTTA WAIT, YOU GOTTA WAIT.

There's a time to sleep and a time to rise,
A time to live and a time to die.
A time to plant a tiny seed,
And harvest it in time of need.

YOU GOTTA WAIT, YOU GOTTA WAIT.

A time to demolish the garden shed,
And build a conservatory instead,
A time for sadness, you cry one day,
A time to dance the night away.

YOU GOTTA WAIT, YOU GOTTA WAIT.

A time when you need somone's care,
A time when you want no one there.

A time to keep the 'dear John' letter,
And rip it up when things get better.

YOU GOTTA WAIT, YOU GOTTA WAIT.

A time to talk with your friends,
A time to sew and a time to mend.
A time to hate all that's wrong,
A time to heal with a peaceful song.

YOU GOTTA WAIT, YOU GOTTA WAIT.

You've gotta wait on God, He's always there,
He is listening for your prayer.
You gotta wait on Him as your strong tower,
You gotta wait on His spirit to give you the power.
You need His light to see things right,
You gotta walk by faith and not by sight.

YOU GOTTA WAIT, YOU GOTTA WAIT.

He knows all about your fears,
He has counted all your tears.
He even counts the hairs on your head,
He knows the day when you'll be dead.
Until that time you live your days,
Giving Him the thanks and praise.

YOU GOTTA WAIT, YOU GOTTA WAIT.

Jesus waited patiently,
From eternity to set us free.
He waited for His Father to speak to Him,
Before He preached about our sin.
He waited for the cross He knew would come,
He showed He was the obedient Son.
Through His death we can know peace,

He is now our great high priest.
In all we do or think or say,
We wait for Him to show the way.

YOU GOTTA WAIT, YOU GOTTA WAIT.

If you're going through some testing,
If you're looking for some blessing,
You can ask for gifts from Him,
To overcome the power of sin.
For He sits at God's right hand,
Through His prayers today we stand.
We wait for Him to come again,
Until that day we say He reigns,
There'll be an end to pain and hate,
Until that day the Church must wait.

BIRDS

This rap provides a stimulus for other ideas of raps about other Bible animals. I simply took a theme 'birds', and looked up all the references to birds in a chain reference Bible. I wanted to introduce the dove as the symbol of the Holy Spirit for Pentecost. I thought it best to do this by getting everyone to think about birds in general. The rap can be used more effectively if you make a rod puppet of a dove which appears in the last verse. The puppet who presents the rap appears with a pair of plastic binoculars around its neck.

God made birds, there's lots to see,
To study them is ornithology.
You put some bins to your eyes,
And watch them flying in the sky.
Buy some books about their eggs,

Colours of feathers, beaks and legs.
Ducks and waders, birds of prey,
So many birds to watch each day.

BIRDS FLY IN THE SKY.

Jesus watched the birds of the air,
He said like them we shouldn't care.
Every bird has its nest,
Jesus had nowhere to rest.
Every sparrow which falls and dies,
Is not hidden from God's eyes.
Birds eat insects, fruit and seed,
God supplies their every need.

GOD FEEDS BIRDS SEEDS.

In the Bible, God's true Word,
We read about all kinds of birds.
Cormorants and pigeons, swallows and hawks,
Owls, herons, thrushes, vultures and storks.
The Israelites caught quail in a net,
Ravens fed Elijah the hungry prophet.
Of all the birds we know and love,
Christians talk about the dove.

THE BIRD IN THE WORD.

When the Lord Jesus was baptized,
A dove descended from the skies.
The Spirit of God is like a dove,
Pure and free, sent from above.
The Spirit is given to all who believe,
The Spirit wants to be received.
So when we see this gentle bird,
We remember the promise of God's Word.

PURE DOVE, GOD'S LOVE.

APPENDIX

This list is in no way comprehensive; some of the books may be difficult to find. You can order them through your local library or from suppliers of puppet books.

USEFUL NAMES AND ADDRESSES

Suppliers of puppets and puppet patterns

Children Worldwide,
'Dalesdown',
Honeybridge Lane,
Dial Post,
Horsham,
West Sussex RH13 8NX
Tel. 0403 710712

David Illiffe is committed to children's evangelism. He literally does travel worldwide and has a selection of books on puppetry and distributes 'Puppets in Praise' puppet patterns internationally.

Ray Da Silva,
The Limes,
Norwich Road,
Marsham
Norfolk NR10 5PS
Tel. 0263 733882

Ray has a quite staggering number of books and items for sale.

The Puppet Centre Trust,
BAC,
176 Lavender Hill
London SW11 5TN

This centre is excellent. They produce a puppet information pack called *Alive an' Kickin'* which has good practical ideas.

David Rockall Puppet
   Theatres,
39 St George's Road,
Worthing BN11 2DR

David designed the puppet theatre whose plan is included in the book. He has other ideas to help you and will make you a theatre at reasonable cost.

Courses on puppetry

London School of Puppetry,
2 Legard Road,
London N5 1DE
Tel. 071-359 7357

This is run by Ronnie Le Drew and Caroline Astell-Birt. They run comprehensive courses.

The Puppet Place
Hengrove School (Room u1),
Petherton Gardens,
Hengrove,
Bristol BS14 9BU
Tel. 0275 838800

Polka Children's Theatre,
240 The Broadway,
Wimbledon,
London SW19
Tel. 081-542 4258

The Puppet Theatre Barge,
Blomfield Road,
Little Venice,
London W9
Tel. 071-249 6876

Scottish Mask & Puppet Centre,
8 Balcarres Avenue,
Kelvindale,
Glasgow G12 0QF
Tel. 041-339 6185

Puppet theatres

Norwich Puppet Theatre,
St James,
Whitefriars,
Norwich NR3 1TN
Tel. 0603 629921

Little Angel Theatre,
14 Dagmar Passage,
London N1 2DN
Tel. 071-226 1787

Cannon Hill Puppet Theatre,
Midlands Arts Centre,
Cannon Hill Park,
Birmingham 12
Tel. 021-440 4221

I've been to this one. It was great.

Books

Roland Sylvester, *Teaching Bible Stories More Effectively with Puppets,* Concordia, USA 1976
Also *Puppets and the Word.* Concordia, St Louis, USA 1983
Dale and Liz Vonseggan, *Puppets-Ministry Magic,* Group Books, Loveland Co., USA 1990
Edited by Everett Robertson, *Using puppetry in the church,* 1976
Also *Puppet scripts for use in church,* Broadman Press, Nashville, Tennessee. Obtainable from The Church Recreation Dept, 127 Ninth Avenue North, Nashville, Tn. 37234 USA

General reading

Caroline Astell-Birt, *Puppetry for mentally handicapped people*, Souvenir Press 1981

Giselda Bittleston, *The healing art of glove puppetry*, Floris Books, Edinburgh 1987

Forman Brown, *Small Wonder,* Scarecrow Press Inc., Metuchen, USA 1980

David Currell, *The Complete Book of the Puppet Theatre,* A. & C. Black, London 1983

Larry Engler & Carol Fynn, *Making Puppets Come Alive,* David & Charles, Newton Abbott 1973

Helen Fling, *Marionettes: How to Make and Work Them,* Dover Publications Inc., New York 1973

Ann Hogarth & Jan Bussell, *Fanfare for Puppets,* David & Charles, London 1985

Robert Leach, *The Punch and Judy Show,* Batsford, London 1985

Janet Lynch-Watson, *The Shadow Puppet Book,* London/New York 1980

Brenda Morton, *Sleeve Puppets,* Faber & Faber, London 1978

A. R. Philpott, *Dictionary of Puppets,* MacDonald, London 1969

Also *Modern Puppetry*, MacDonald, London 1966

George Speaight, *The History of the English Puppet Theatre,* G. Harrap & Co., London 1955

M. von Bohen, *Dolls and puppets,* G. Harrap & Co., London 1932

Lindy Wright, *Puppets,* Franklin Watts, London 1987

If you contact the Church Army they will tell you who amongst their officers is currently involved in puppetry.

Songs for use
with scripts

Zacchaeus

Calypso style - Freely

Words and Music by Stuart Holt

Zac - chae - us climbed the tree that day so he could clear - ly see Je - sus the Son of God who came to set us free. May we too be in the place to clear - ly see the

Lord of Lords

Words and music by Stuart Holt

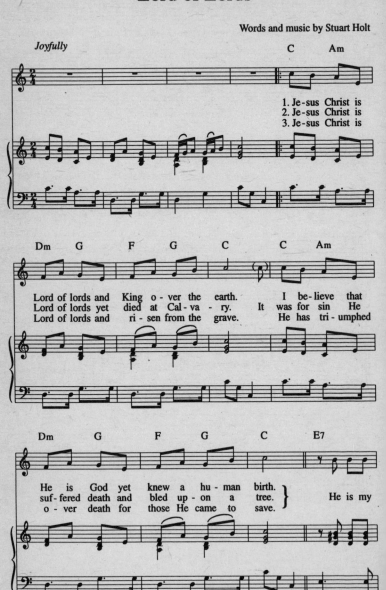

1. Je-sus Christ is Lord of lords and King o-ver the earth. I be-lieve that He is God yet knew a hu-man birth. He is my
2. Je-sus Christ is Lord of lords yet died at Cal-va-ry. It was for sin He suf-fered death and bled up-on a tree.
3. Je-sus Christ is Lord of lords and ri-sen from the grave. He has tri-umphed o-ver death for those He came to save.

Sa - viour,—— He died for me. Je-sus Christ is

Lord of lords and He has set me free.

▼▲▼▲▼▲▼▲▼▲▼▲▼▲▼▲▼▲▼▲▼▲▼▲▼▲▼▲▼▲▼▲▼▲▼▲

I will search for my sheep

Words and music by Stuart Holt

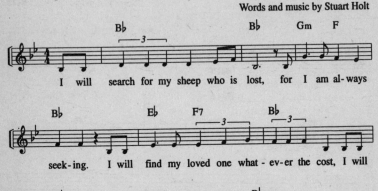

I will search for my sheep who is lost, for I am al-ways

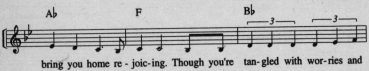

seek-ing. I will find my loved one what-ev-er the cost, I will

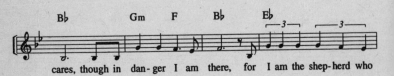

bring you home re-joic-ing. Though you're tan-gled with wor-ries and

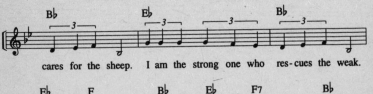

cares, though in dan-ger I am there, for I am the shep-herd who

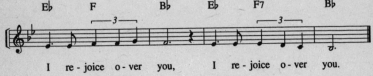

cares for the sheep. I am the strong one who res-cues the weak.

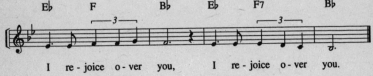

I re-joice o-ver you, I re-joice o-ver you.

Have mercy on me

Words and music by Stuart Holt

Joyfully

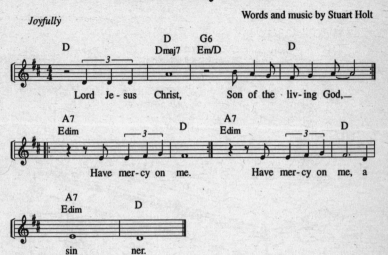

Lord Je - sus Christ, Son of the liv-ing God,—

Have mer-cy on me.

Have mer-cy on me, a

sin ner.

Plan for making a puppet theatre

VIEW ON ARROW 'A'

2 HOLES
35mm DIA

GROOVE
3mm WIDE X 8mm DEEP

17

45

45

22

4 No.2" NON-REBATED
HINGES

CURTAIN WIRE RUNNING
FULL LENGTH OF
HINGED FRONT PANEL

100

SPRING CLIP
35mm

'A'

6

1760

1690 CTRS

35

775

OSMA
4Z210
45°/135°

1040

700

1 1/4"OSMA
WELDABLE
WASTE PIPE

OSMA
4Z163
132°

135

OSMA
4Z190
87 1/2° / 92 1/2°

MULTI-FIT
S28M

OSMA
4Z160
90°

1460

55

510

250

CUT TUBE TO DIMENSIONS SHOWN
ALL DIMENSIONS IN MM.
NOT TO SCALE

Simple and easy ideas for puppets

PAPER BAG PUPPETS

Large bags,
use two
hands

Small bag
for single
hand

SHADOW PUPPETS

Fix a line across the room.
Hang up an old white sheet
using clothes pegs. Use
overhead projector or
angle-poise lamp as light
source. Try out well in
advance to ensure shadow
images are effective. Cut
figures etc out of cereal
boxes. Keep outlines
simple for best effects. Fix
spills or garden sticks to
back

WOODEN SPOON PUPPET

Felt tip hair
and features

Material
or paper
gathered
at 'neck'

Limbs of card
may be added

ROD PUPPETS

Moving people

Back view: use card from
cereal boxes and paper
fasteners. Wooden spills
attached with sticky
pads/tape to move head
and limbs

Decorate
with wool,
material scraps etc.

Birds, fish, insects

Use simple
household junk
with rods
(drinking straws
used here)

Animal rod puppets

Use card and yogurt pots for
head. Decorate with wool etc..
Fix rod to head and to body.
Bodies from paper-covered
springs or rope covered with
screwed-up tissue paper

▼▲▼▲▼▲▼▲▼▲▼▲▼▲▼▲▼▲▼▲▼▲▼▲▼▲▼▲▼▲▼▲▼▲▼▲

GLOVE PUPPETS

a) Mould a clay head to fit on first finger. Felt tip features. Pin a handkerchief round hand

b) Make a template larger than hand. Cut out two of shape using felt or scrap material. Add features/hair to one and then sew both together

FINGER PUPPETS

a) Simply paint features/hair onto fingers. Fingerless mittens look good!

b) Use card cylinders and material scraps

PUPPETS ON STRING

Junk head and floaty material make good angels

For two or more strings use coat hangers to aid control

▼▲▼▲▼▲▼▲▼▲▼▲▼▲▼▲▼▲▼▲▼▲▼▲▼▲▼▲▼▲▼▲▼▲▼▲

HAND PUPPETS

(i) With felt or scrap material, make two shapes slightly bigger than hand. This will be the head

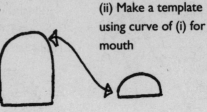

(ii) Make a template using curve of (i) for mouth

(iii) Fold a piece of felt for mouth. Put folded edge on straight edge of template. Draw round and cut. Open out

(iv) Draw/glue/sew features on one head shape

(v) Sew half of mouth to head shape round curve. Sew other half to plain shape. Join up side seams

Operate with fingers at top and thumb as lower jaw

SOCK PUPPETS

Add buttons for eyes. Shape of head can be changed with card or stuffing